Rebecca Gillieron studied Philosophy at Cambridge University. She works as an editor at Marion Boyars Publishers, playing various instruments and singing for bands including wetdog and The Ha-Ha Show in her spare time. She has recently moved to Kent with the intention of building a music/painting studio in the back garden.

Catheryn Kilgarriff studied English & Philosophy at Bristol University and then spent a year at the London College of Printing learning typesetting in hot metal, plate making and the odd bit of computer technology. She worked as a design consultant before taking a leap of faith to become the publisher at Marion Boyars Publishers when Marion Boyars, her mother, became ill in 1999. She lives in London with her husband and teenage daughters.

THE BOOKAHOLICS' GUIDE TO

Book Blogs

Published in 2007 in Great Britain and the United States by
MARION BOYARS PUBLISHERS LTD
24 Lacy Road, London, SW15 1NL

www.marionboyars.co.uk

Distributed in Australia and New Zealand by Tower Books, Pty Ltd,
Unit 2, 17 Rodborough Road, Frenchs Forest, NSW 2086, Australia

Printed in 2007
10 9 8 7 6 5 4 3 2 1

A CIP catalogue record for this book is available from the British Library.
A CIP catalog record for this book is availble from the Library of Congress.

10 digit ISBN: 0 7145 3151 0
13 digit ISBN: 978 0 7145 3151 9

Set in Bembo 11pt
Printed in the UK by CPI Bookmarque, Croydon, CR0 4TD

Cover design by Holly MacDonald.
Cover photograph by Dovegreyreader.

The Bookaholics' Guide To
Book Blogs

by
Rebecca Gillieron
&
Catheryn Kilgarriff

MARION BOYARS PUBLISHERS
LONDON • NEW YORK

Contents

Introduction

You are not alone

A few years back, we all worked at the office or at home, using pens, typewriters and the odd computer, hoping, as publishers, that the authors we found would become successful and that we would be able to persuade a major newspaper to run a review. Readers of new books relied on reviewers, prizes and word of mouth to find the books that they would choose to read.

Then the internet began to take off. At the beginning, in the late 1980s and early 1990s (I was working in a product design consultancy and we were meant to be a state of the art company, advising major corporations on their future destinies), we became aware that there were a few good sites to visit. The BBC was a leader. However, in the small organisations I worked for, even though the projects they worked on were billed in thousands of pounds, it was normal for only one computer in an office to be connected to the internet and email was only checked occasionally. Many good business leads were lost this way, through emails being ignored. I recall that, as a product design business developer, trying to contact the British Telecommunications research department for work, we were told that its futurology department only communicated by email, which we just thought arrogant at the time. But I think they were trying to make the point that they were way ahead of us.

Gradually, email became the way people in offices communicated, which meant we did not have to type faxes out or run up large phone bills. Then people realised it was quite easy to construct their own websites, so it became easier to find out what was happening in other companies.

Then came the blog.

And just like Amazon, the pioneer of online retailing, it seems that books were first in line for blog attention.

Do book lovers blog because they are naturally verbose, or is it that people who love books are essentially quiet loners who like nothing more than working quietly all day in front of a screen, and curling up with a book at home in the evening? If so, the book blog gave readers a chance to break out of the solitary confinement of reading, and reach out to fellow readers. We could visit the blogs of other book lovers every other day, and see what they had been reading and recommending.

No longer is there only one option – book reviews written by badly paid specialists and review space fought over with expensive meals and invitations to champagne galas and book prizes. As a small publisher, it is very rare for us to meet or talk to book reviewers. The whole system by which some books are chosen for review, and others are overlooked, is a mystery to us. However, a new channel has opened up. Today, you can find like-minded people by hunting on the internet and you can communicate by email with blog owners. The book bloggers write their reviews and thoughts on the world of books, authors and publishers because they love books and want to spread the word that they have found a great book.

Independent publishers choose their frontlist out of a genuine enthusiasm and love for a book. It may be a Swedish classic overlooked, as in *The Serious Game* by Hjalmar Söderberg, or *Banquet of Lies* by Amin Zaoui which takes the lid off teenage sexuality and Islam. We try to convince ourselves that our own enthusiasm for a book can be turned into a marketing campaign, but we are not talking currency like the sides of buses or TV adverts. We believe that the book bloggers have started their websites for the same reasons – sheer enthusiasm for the books they have found and read.

Occasionally we ask the blog owners what they find when working with the larger, commercial publishers, and we have heard that they are put on review lists, and sent every single book from a large house anonymously. This makes them feel like an Orwellian bit-part player from *1984* rather than an appreciated commentator. At the same time, the bloggers have found that print literary journalists are less than complimentary about the value of their output. So, it is fitting that an independent publishing house should choose to capture the moment when book bloggers have not become addenda to the normal practise of creating literary heavyweight titles, the BIG ones which we are always told we should be creating.

This book is meant to capture this moment, it's a book blog keepsake, when book blogs are exploding across the web and in it we talk about the ones who are good, who should be sought out, communicated with and encouraged. It is also a discussion about the nature of the internet and how it has changed our expectations about how we receive information. The problems of who information belongs to are also part of this discussion, since there are some very large players who would like to have access to all the content and information in the world, regardless of how or by whom it was created.

Our role

We're a publishing house, albeit a slightly idealistic one. We work in a terraced house in Putney, surrounded by shelves full of books from the backlist, holes in the carpet, our shiny Apple Macs which are connected to each other by wi fi (which sometimes works and sometimes doesn't – why this should be is a mystery to us) but essentially we spend our time choosing, chasing, editing, designing and marketing our smallish list, sometimes choosing to commission books rather than waiting for good ideas to come to us. We never really know if we are making the right choices. This time we decided to write a book ourselves since the presence of all those book bloggers makes us feel less lonely and isolated. We wanted to celebrate this new community of like-minded souls and since the internet is a transient thing, we didn't want the existence of some of the first book bloggers to come and go without a record.

Before we start though, I should insert a quick note about the inevitable pitfalls. There are thousands of bloggers online who really do 'live books', who work in the book trade as writers, reviewers or booksellers, and it will not be possible to include them all. As we are a publishing house, we gravitate towards the ones we know and who have similarities with us. We also find that the literary establishment is full of creativity and ideas and we celebrate the people in it who have joined in with this irresistible community. In fact I am surprised that more literary editors do not join in. It's comforting, elucidating, erudite and fun to join the community of bloggers. It must be a little like being a shy teenager at the dance, resisting the lure of the blog and not joining in. So I apologise in advance to anyone who may feel slighted at being left out of this book, and I can only urge you to compile your own volume to make up for our omissions.

The book blog sites which we refer to throughout this book are often written by people we know in the trade, and have met at the many social events we attend. Book fairs, award ceremonies and parties (if we are lucky enough to be invited), missions to other countries to look for books in translation, sales conferences (these are incredibly sociable events when you are a small publisher being sold and distributed by a company with over eighty other small publishers) are just some of these events. However, many excellent blogs are written by people who wish to remain anonymous and who have come to enjoy the interplay between book lover and book professional. All these people have a deep love of – if not obsession with – books, which is where the bookaholics of the title of this book came from. Another of the great levellers in book blogs is that they are almost all written exclusively by one person. Even on a publisher's blog, different contributors sign their work. This means that the views on blogs are personal, free from censorship and from the heart. In them, you can find exactly what people think of books and the way they are sold.

Catheryn Kilgarriff

Jumping on the Bandwagon

Individuals who blog

To my way of thinking, the best book bloggers are individuals who have no grist or motive other than a love of books and a desire to share their finds with others.

In this category, I will also place some authors, as writers often blog for other reasons than to promote their own writing (they are actually quite bashful about this – we find it very hard to persuade many of our writers to give us their author photographs to use for promotion – we have to ask several times and invent pressing deadlines in order for one to appear. Then, their next question when we see them is always: 'How did you use it?' or 'May I see, please?'. Self-promotion can be a difficult matter.) Authors maintain blogs because they wish to keep in touch with like-minded people, and their readers. I think they know that they are not going to do anything other than be easier to approach by having a blog. They will not become rich overnight, or win the Man Booker prize. But they may hear directly from their readers. It is actually quite difficult as a writer to know what people think of your work, mainly because people are shy of letting their feelings be known.

As a publisher, I also have little idea of how our books are received, except I know I enjoy publishing them, and enough people buy them to pay the bills that a small company needs to pay. I did get a little insight recently, when I read on a forum about a launch we did for *Chocolate and Zucchini*. There, I could read that the room in the Institut Français in South Kensington was lovely (yes, I had bothered to bring flowers), that the author, Clotilde Dusoulier, was pretty (that I knew) and that some of the food I had cooked from her recipe book was felt to be sublime, and also that the fact Jude Law was in the building on the same night was considered a coup.

This person had not noticed that a bottle of champagne exploded over the hazelnut bread sticks, making them soggy, that the food was left for people to help themselves to as we did not have waiting staff, and the slide equipment was not quite ready in time. These details I read about on another blog, by someone else who had been there. Ah well – we can't be perfect. The point I am making is that blogs open people up to both praise and criticism, and the internet is an open forum in which opinions can be raised. There is no need for resources such as the ones we have here, which enable the printing of books. The internet is an ideal medium for individuals to express their opinions and engage in lively debate.

The fact is that most individuals start blogging for no commercial reason whatsoever. They are just drawn to their subject, and have found that the blog is a perfect tool for making their passion known.

My all-time favourite person to check in on is Dovegreyreader. We have used a photograph from her site on the cover. It is one of many piles of books which she posts on her site, so we can see what she is either reading, or is contemplating reading, since no one could possibly read all the books she mentions in her postings.

Dovegreyreader is a part-time nurse (with many years full-time service, no doubt) who lives in rural Devon and has a serious book habit. We get occasional glimpses of her book shelves and her craft projects, and a few of the fields and cows surrounding her home. We also get more than a few photographs of her cat.

Dovegreyreader's book taste usually tallies with my own and I have often agreed with her when she is critical (she did not like *Suite Française* and thought it was a book that benefited from huge hype. I thought it worthy but a very familiar style of book, concentrating on a few episodes to explain a very complicated and tragic occurrence – the treatment of Jewish families in wartime France.). She also had wonderful comments on the use of the 'wrong' suitcase on the cover. This response highlights a frequent pitfall of publishers – we have to hunt quickly for cover images and we sometimes make mistakes. For example, we used the wrong kind of bee on our cover for *Four Walls* by Vangelis Hatziyannidis – they are bumblebees, not honey bees, which are the mousy kind of worker bees no one ever draws in school. I read about our sin on a book blog, of course.

Dovegreyreader's opinions can also be useful for situations where you read a book you do not entirely enjoy, but which she has enthused about. This is the case with an Orange Prize shortlisted book from independent Tindal Street Press, *What Was Lost* by Catherine O'Flynn. I was not bowled over by the start, but because of Dovegreyreader's praise, I have persevered and the original writing is now shining through for me as well. However, here she is on Amelie Nothomb, a writer I have not yet read myself, but one day will thanks to Dovegreyreaders's enthusiasm:

> *Fear and Trembling* was the first one I opened (no I didn't read it in French but you can) and immediately I was plunged into the strange world of Japanese corporate life seen through the eyes of a Westerner and surely a barely disguised account of Amelie Nothomb's own experience? Amelie is employed for a year as the office dogsbody but clearly has talents far in excess of those required. For openers her fluent Japanese causes dismay amongst the clients and she is asked to forget it and pretend she doesn't understand.
>
> Humiliated and constantly demoted to increasingly menial tasks as a punishment for showing intuition and common sense beyond the ken of her employers, Amelie spends the final few months of her employment cleaning the toilets. Of course this backfires spectacularly on the occupants of the offices on the

44th floor who are then too embarrassed to use them so have to waste valuable company time trekking off to those on the 43rd floor. It hardly sounds like enough to make a novel but Amelie Nothomb does just that, presenting a world that appears by turns, both funny and ridiculous if it wasn't quite so frighteningly serious and just possibly true.

I have no idea whether this is an accurate representation of Japanese corporate life or a caricature and wonder whether any of my Japanese visitors here might be able to enlighten me? Whatever, this was a great read and I'm up for more Amelie Nothomb which is fortunate as I bought four.

Since starting her blog in March 2006, Dovegreyreader has been found by many publishers and her site is now swamped with books which they have sent to her. As long as her site remains online her posts will be a reference point for some of the best publishing by the independent presses of the UK, who are a small and brave group. I also like Dovegreyreader's relationship with the French language, which does not appear to intimidate her.

We know from her attitude to holidays that she is just as happy to stay at home as to jump on a plane. One of her favourite holidays was a cruise in the Bahamas which included a 3000 volume floating library, although she also took a suitcase of books with her in case they were the wrong 3000 books. But when a book is a translation from the French, Dovegreyreader is instantly attracted since she knows she could, at a pinch, read the original. Another of my favourite posts on her site is from a visiting friend who is invited to many of the parties, prizes and jamborees Dovegreyreader enjoys and comments on the outfits worn by the authors and famous editors. You'll have to go to her site and find this for yourselves. I did originally fantasise about submitting photographs to Dovegreyreader from parties I went to, but when the moment comes, I am far too busy to actually remember to do this so I have totally failed to augment this fascinating gallery with fashion shots from the *Independent* Foreign Fiction Prize. Just let me add that there is a skirt in my wardrobe which I will not wear to any bookish party since I know that an editor at Sphere has the exact same one although fortunately we have not both worn it to the same party. I'll have to be careful this does not happen in the future.

In the realm of author sites which I love, I would place Laila Lalami, whose site is named Moorish Girl, near the top. I like this site as Lalami is a Moroccan and often spends time there, although her main residence is in the US. I'm attracted to the distant and different and I do become a bit bored with posts which are entirely Soho-based, no matter how amusing I may find them. She is also an up-and-coming writer and has her eye on the book world fairly keenly. The following post, from March 2005, shows how her blog is being read by other writers and commented on. This blog came about because of an article appearing in February 2005 in *The Times* by AS Byatt, a well known British writer and the sister of Margaret Drabble.

> AS Byatt is quoted in *The Times* as saying that it's time to change the way in which used books are sold. Dame Antonia Byatt has called for new rules to protect novelists using a system known as *droit de suite*, which guarantees artists a payment for each subsequent sale of their work. The rule is already scheduled to be introduced for visual art next year to ensure that painters receive a payment for second-hand sales of their work.
>
> Michael at The Literary Saloon weighs in on the issue, bringing up the question of whether authors should worry about money from used books or about having more readers:
>
> > Sadly, of course, the answer is simple: authors only want money and care about having readers only insofar as not having any eventually generally – though, given how the publishing industry works nowadays, not always – prevents them from

> raking in any cash. (No emails, please, we know you (whoever you are) are the shining, beneficent exception.)

I would only add that in countries without a giant publishing industry and where readership is limited for various reasons (that is to say, a large part of the world) most authors have no expectation that their book sales will make them a living, much less afford them the luxury to write full-time. For these authors, whether a book is sold new or used is essentially irrelevant. They write because they have something to say, not because someone is paying them a ridiculously large advance. Readers continue to respond to this post, and its follow-up, about whether authors should get royalties on used books. Colleen Mondor, Children's Book Review Editor at Eclectica, who worked in a used bookstore in Alaska for two years, weighs in on the logistical problems raised by a subsequent-royalties system of the kind that AS Byatt wants:

> In the larger stores (Powells, Strand, etc.) employees inventory by title, regardless of new or used, but in most used stores the used books are all lumped together by the 'Used' category...we had no idea what we had by title as far as the inventory system was concerned. So in order to compensate authors we would have to inventory every used book by title as they came in, keeping in mind that a large number of them do not have ISBN codes, and then what? Notify publishers that we have the book? Or do we notify them only after we sell the book? When purchasing new books, it is all done up front, when the store buys the book from the wholesaler (like Ingram). But how would this used process work? As I check out the new and used bookstores in my town now, I see various displays of books from a hundred years old to six months ago...and some are sold by hand receipt that merely states 'books' under the description. How do you keep track of that by title? And who keeps this whole mess honest? Quite simply, the system does not exist for most stores to accommodate the sort of

> tracking that some authors (Byatt) seem to want. And that is how it is in the used world. Do you think Ford gets a cut from used trucks sold at the local street corner car lot? Do fashion designers get money from thrift store sales or record companies from the used record stores? It doesn't happen because it would be insane to try and do. I'm not even going to start on how chaotic the pricing standards would be. A book that sells in Florida for $10 might get only $1 in Alaska...same condition, but the subject matter demands a higher price in one locale as opposed to another. Would authors be happy with such haphazard pricing?

Powell's David Weich is similarly sceptical of subsequent-royalty schemes.

> New books get sold, not leased. The implicit contract of such an exchange transfers ownership to the buyer; whether it's a book or a painting or a couch or a dog or a rock that has been sold, the purchaser now 'owns' it. At that point, the artist or toy maker or craftsman has ceded control over the product. I don't buy into the idea that a writer's product is any different, or more valuable, than that of any craftsperson. It strikes me as self-righteous and belittling of others' work. If a publisher were to resell a book's content – the issue has come up in various forms over digital republication rights – then the writer may very well have a legitimate claim to additional compensation. However, if a writer were due compensation every time his/her book is resold, the value of the item would immediately decrease; in effect, the original bookstore customer is paying for a different product: a product with no resale rights. And this arrangement isn't particular to the book industry; it's the basis of our economy. Should the maker of my desk lamp get a cut when I resell it at a yard sale?

Comparisons between books and other products also form the basis of reader Ken Bronson's response:

> I first heard this argument that content originators should get compensation for sales on used items when Garth Brooks made the case that musicians and songwriters should get money for used CDs. I don't get how a book or a CD or a movie is different from a car or a toaster. I can sell my car and Chrysler won't get a kickback. I never really researched why artists think they are selling something different than toasters. Sorry but no one has ever explained it in a way that makes sense to me.
>
> Since books have been compared here with used trucks, CDs, desk lamps and toasters, I feel compelled to point out a couple of things. There is a difference between books as art objects and books as products. When taken as art objects, books don't have a monetary value and cannot be quantified in the same way. Books are not written according to a specific set of independently verifiable features. Our reactions to them are entirely subjective – we may love them or hate them. They can make us laugh or cry; they can reshape our views of life or leave us thoroughly untouched; they can make us happy or so angry that we issue fatwas over their authors.
>
> However, when a book is sold to a publisher, when it has an ISBN, a nice cover by Chip Kidd, a fancy author photo by Marion Ettlinger, and a price tag, it becomes a product, indistinguishable from other products on store shelves. The expectation that it should be treated any differently strikes me as a little absurd.

There are a plethora of sites which have the word 'book' in them, and I find it rather hard to keep up with all of them. But here is Bookninja – which sounds to me like a person who can read a book and do karate at the same time, but is actually a blog run by two writers and editors George Murray and Katherine Kuitenbrouwer – on the issue of 'choosing the best' young novelists. Bookninja has a few pithy remarks about the criteria used. I first heard of the Granta hunt for the top twenty under-forty American young novelists in the office of the *New York Review of Books,* in October 2006, when I was visiting New York. The owner of the *New York Review of Books*, Rea Elderman, had recently sold Granta to Sigrid Rausing, multi millionaire Tetra Pak heiress. My honest opinion is that it is really hard to achieve 'best' status when you are under forty, since not only do your books have to be published in the US, they also should have crossed over into the UK. The UK book market is an incredibly difficult one. We have found that publishing radical New York writers almost always backfires. We would have nominated Arthur Nersesian, a writer who has been nurtured by Brooklyn-based Akashic Books. *Chinese Takeout* is a book that had been reprinted several times, was adored in New York and enjoyed a modest amount of success in the UK, but was only really taken up by the book buyers at Waterstone's Piccadilly. But my main point here is that Arthur Nersesian's fortieth birthday has come and gone, so alas, he will not benefit from the blast of publicity that being included in Granta's top forty allows.

So here is what Bookninja has to say about the selection process for the top twenty under-forty American writers:

> **Funny Thing**
> What ever happened to being funny? I bet seriousness runs in inverse proportion to the level of hardship experienced by the readership. As we get richer, fatter and more leisurely, we prefer to get our tragedy vicariously. Were we starving and the proud owners of a 35 year lifespan and a 40% infant mortality rate, we just might need a few chuckles…
>
> Two things were striking about the twenty-five [sic] writers recently anointed by *Granta* magazine as America's 'best young novelists'. The first is that nearly all of them are graduates of university creative writing courses. The second is that they are a uniformly depressive, angst-ridden lot.
>
> In his summing-up essay, *Granta*'s editor Ian Jack remarked

upon this second fact: 'We read many books infused by loss and a feeling that present things would not go on for ever, written by people whose age put them at a distance from their own mortality.' Jack went on to lament the exclusion from the list of Joshua Ferris, who 'had the singular distinction...of making me laugh aloud quite often.'

In other words, of the twenty 'best' young novelists in America, not one is producing work that makes people laugh. Isn't this more than a little peculiar? It isn't as if the comic novel doesn't have a distinguished pedigree.

Foer doesn't make people laugh? Um? And it continues, in much greater depth, in a *Prospect* magazine essay by Julian Gough:

> Yet western culture since the middle ages has overvalued the tragic and undervalued the comic. We think of tragedy as major, and comedy as minor. Brilliant comedies never win the best film Oscar. The Booker Prize leans toward the tragic. In 1984, Martin Amis reinvented Rabelais in his comic masterpiece *Money*. The best English novel of the 1980s, it didn't even make the shortlist. Anita Brookner won that year, for *Hotel du Lac*, written, as the *Observer* put it, 'with a beautiful grave formality.'

The fault is in the culture. But it is also internalised in the writers, who self-limit and self-censor. If the subject is big, difficult and serious, the writer tends to believe the treatment must be in the tragic mode. When Amis addressed the Holocaust in his minor novel *Time's Arrow* (1991), he switched off the jokes, and the energy, and was rewarded with his only Booker shortlisting.

But why this pressure, from within and without? There are two good reasons. The first is the West's unexamined cultural cringe before the Greeks. For most of the last 500 years, Homer

> and Sophocles have been held to be the supreme exponents of their arts. (Even Homer's constant repetition of stock phrases like 'rosy-fingered dawn' and 'wine-dark sea' are praised, rather than recognised as tiresome clichés.)
>
> The second reason is that our classical inheritance is lopsided. We have a rich range of tragedies – Sophocles, Aeschylus and Euripides (eighteen by Euripides alone). Of the comic writers, only Aristophanes survived. In an age of kings, time is a filter that works against comedy. Plays that say, 'Boy, it's a tough job, leading a nation' tend to survive; plays that say, 'Our leaders are dumb arseholes, just like us' tend not to.
>
> More importantly, Aristotle's work on tragedy survived; his work on comedy did not. We have the classical rules for the one but not the other, and this has biased the development of all western literature. We've been off-centre ever since.

So here already we have examples of people who are book lovers, booksellers, writers and book buyers, and they all seem to have sensible points to make about how bestsellers rise to the top, the criteria on which 'best of' lists are generated, and how come good, sarcastic writers rarely make the Booker shortlist. Where in the world of literary pages in print would we find articles like these?

Catheryn Kilgarriff

Alter Egos or Inflated Egos? Why Do People Blog?

Me, me, ME!

Since the phenomena emerged we have seen blogs from singletons hoping the net's web will find them a soul mate, blogs from rock stars on tour round the world, blogs from NHS doctors on their daily rounds, blogs from out-of-work actors, blogs from hugely successful football players, there are even kiddie-blogs from net savvy schoolchildren detailing the minutiae of their 4th form existence. But not all blogs are of the 'me, me, me' variety. Though many may find it hard to deflect criticism that they are self-obsessed, deluded fools with no social skills, too much time on their hands, too many opinions or too much trivia on their brains with nowhere but their own web portals to air it, it is fair to say that the majority of book bloggers, at least, are not of this ilk.

That the altruistic nature of the book blogger warrants considerable admiration may be self-evident (these people really do care about the material they are dealing with and blog simply for the pleasure of passing on information about their reading experiences, good and bad), but it is worth commenting also on the nature of the 'beast' this altruism directs itself towards. We're not talking about blogs on bad pop music or celebrity bitching here, which can be trivial and even exhausting (though not always!). These bloggers are well-informed bibliophiles seeking to promote an activity that stimulates thought, encourages self-reliance, harms no one else and is not damaging to our health in any way: READING. These people aren't using the internet to encourage cannibalism, self-harm, suicide or simple hedonism. It's a love of literature we're talking about here. How could you *not* be in favour?

Outsiders and the ideal of independent vision

The fact is that many do object. The issue is not just the debate over 'reviews in print vs reviews on the internet' (though we return to this in Chapter 9). Questions are raised about the individuals themselves. Who are these people? Are they *really* as altruistic as they make out? Why do they think they have useful opinions to offer? Why should we care about what they think of the latest bestsellers anyhow?

When a blogger such as UK Bookseller to the Stars (see Chapter 4) Mark Farley sets himself the torturous task of reading one ghost-written celebrity biography a week (apparently to help him understand the irritating success of this phenomena) you can't help but wonder what it's all about. And what of the online reading group which challenges members to pluck out a book from the shelves each weekend, that they own but don't want to read, and forcing themselves to read it? WHY?! With nutcases like this on the airwaves – or internet equivalent, spot the technical wizard – its hardly surprising that the validity of these self-elected critics may be subject to scrutiny. (Actually, I quite like the idea of forcing yourself to read something you hate, but this is besides the point...)

The business of reviews

The classic objection is that with newspapers and print publications, at least the editors have endorsed a critic's opinion, endowing it with an authority that the critic is meant to have somehow earned. In theory, this 'earning' process is achieved through prior experience of reviewing, there may be evidence of he or she 'being right' about a particularly successful book or books in the past perhaps. But isn't all artistic judgement subjective? Don't we accept that the merits of a play, a painting or a work of literary fiction might not adhere to hard and fast rules that can be used to measure their worth? In which case why do we listen to these people at all, let alone allow them to guide our purchases and preferences?

Perhaps this is looking at things from the wrong angle. Ignoring rating systems that use asterisk symbols for the time being, it seems the whole process of reviewing is not a question of giving 'grades' to authors or putting them in categories accordingly. We are not looking to be spoon-fed supposedly objective judgements about the worth of an artwork, piece of music or book. We just want an insight into someone else's *subjective* viewpoints, in order to save us wasting our time with cultural experiences we know we will not like. It is arguable that we look to critics to find others with opinions a little like our own. When they repeatedly guide us to books that we enjoy, we return for more information about what they are reading, for more guidance on what we will enjoy reading. We like to hear them agree with our opinions. We like to disagree with some of their opinions (in order to feed our own egos in some cases but also to remind ourselves we have our own views). But we are aware that they cannot be called 'right' or 'wrong' in their evaluation of something, any more than we could be.

It is likely that the reader-reviewer relationship is more of a two-way relationship than the average critic might be willing to allow. Maybe we influence the critics' choices as much as they do ours. When the readers like what the critics are producing, and the critics get good feedback, more hits on their websites, more work from the newspaper that employs them, then in turn the critic may tailor their responses to a book or their choices of titles to review, according to these fluctuating tastes.

Alter egos or inflated egos?

That book bloggers are particularly suited to their task, may be a result of their unique awareness of this relationship. As avid readers who seek to share their opinions, without the motivation of monetary gain, without a particular remit, house style or editorial policy to fit in with, they are placed in direct contact with other readers and bloggers who discuss each other's responses to a book on a daily basis. The interaction is immediate. The discourse unfettered. The reason we should care about what these people say is the simple fact that they are saying it without restriction. Without intermediary editorial processes that may dilute the message that they wish to spread. If you are dealing with just one individual, sitting merrily in their living room armed with a laptop, there are no booksellers or publishers pushing particular titles that may prejudice the choice of reviews in the way that newspapers and magazines may be affected (although as bloggers begin to sell advertising space and/or books from their sites this may well be changing already).

Time and time again the same response arises. Why do people blog about books? Because they want people to enjoy the same literature that they enjoy. Because they want to talk about this literature that they enjoy. Because they want this literature to receive the attention it deserves, and the mainstream publishing world may not be giving it due credit. Of course there are those bloggers who enjoy the reputation that they build for themselves on the internet and those whose egos are bigger than their personalities or opinions deserve. But the overriding motivation, from the outset at least, is not about self-promotion for the majority. At the risk of making sweeping generalisations, it seems fair to say that altruism is the name of the game here.

As Golden Rule Jones explains (see the Lit Blog Co-op Blog

2005) often bloggers just want to do the work that they realise needs to be done:

> I see blogging as a way to take up what Walter Benjamin called 'the struggle against dispersion,' and to find my own answer to the question posed by the Swiss writer Robert Walser: 'Assuredly there exists...work of the kind that one can do as in a dream?'
>
> In other words, some of it (like my events list) is work that needs to be done that no one else is doing. Why do you have to live in Chicago for ten years before you know what the heck is going on? And have to browse thousands of self-help author events just to find the one night Adam Zagajewski will be in Chicago in your lifetime? Crazy.
>
> The rest is just me following my own impulses, without deadlines or commitments or ambitions or any expectation of return.

In fact in this same post Golden Rule Jones even points out the fact that he really isn't interested in gaining a reputation, quite the opposite:

> (I blog under a pseudonym, so even the small notoriety I've earned from the blog doesn't accrue to me. Which is perfect.)

The founder of Bookgasm also explains that the reason he writes a book blog is to take care of work that he feels needs doing (and commenting on the sheer enjoyment he gets from the blog):

> My whole impetus for starting Bookgasm was because I was frustrated at not being able to find reviews or discussion about the kind of books I was interested in reading, particularly the genre stuff like horror. So I thought I'd just do it myself, because someone needed to fill that void. I know there are lots of sites out there that discuss such books, but most are not from a level of professionalism

> or legitimacy, whereas I'm a working journalist. I'd like to think we provide a service. I have a lot of fun doing Bookgasm – so much that I wish I could devote my entire day to it.

Rod Lott of Bookgasm was also kind enough to point us in the direction of the Emerging Writers Forum, whose website (www.breaktech.net) features a great interview from Dan Wickett who speaks to various literary bloggers about why they blog – amongst other things. This is definitely worth a read, but I'll include a few quotes here that emphasise the fun aspect of blogging as well as flagging up the desire to share.

Cupcake from cupcakeseries.com writes:

> We thought other people – lots of other people, we suspected - would have something interesting to say about issues we thought important and valid as well, and that starting a blog would be a fun way to talk about what we like to talk about, even more.

Not everyone is in it for the sake of others. In this same feature, Michael of the Literary Saloon admits:

> I am the primary intended audience (along with the rest of the Complete Review 'staff'): I look for and post the information that is of interest to me.

To be fair, Michael's later explanation of his motivations place him in a better light, when he states that he started his blog:

> a) to find out about books that might be of interest to me
> b) to inform readers about books, authors, and literary events that might be of interest to them, and
> c) to entertain visitors

But it's comments from Megan of Bookdwarf that put the altruism of book bloggers firmly back in the picture

> I want to write for anyone who reads books, although I sometimes fear I end up being read by friends and family only. I would definitely like it if someone reading my site were to find a new author or a new book they wouldn't have without me.

For Megan, it's a simple matter of promoting good literature to people who care:

> I want to expand coverage of books beyond the popular ones. If I like a book I'll talk about it, but especially if I think the *Times* or other lit-bloggers have missed it, I want to encourage people to read it more. There's not as much I can add to the discussion about a book that's got a hundred reviews already.

I think I've made my point. But just to round this section off here's one last quote from Golden Rule Jones again, that I have to admit gets me all emotional:

> High-horse time: To me, literature doesn't live in books. It lives in the community of people who read them, think about them, and talk about them. The conversation that occurs around literary works – a living conversation that began centuries ago and includes, in its most public forms, both Samuel Johnson and the guy who reviewed Robinson's *Gilead* in the *New York Times* last week – is in the end what distinguishes these works from the average chunky paperback you read to make a flight seem shorter. Participating in that conversation – even in this tiny, evanescent way – delights the hell out of me.

These people really do care. Thumbs up to them all!

The online persona

One of the most interesting things about book bloggers is the peculiar identities that they choose for themselves. The alter egos, pseudonyms and personas that these people adopt not only define their online existence but can be nothing short of fantastic in some instances. Of course there are those that have no illusions about themselves, 'Grumpy Old Bookman' is hardly casting himself in the most flattering light, neither are 'Bourgeouis Nerd' or 'Old Hag' and some might be put off for quite different reasons by the self-proclaimed 'Bookslut' or 'Fiction Bitch'. But when the whole enterprise of running a book blog is designed to make readers sit up and take notice of what you have to say, can anyone be blamed for adopting a *nom de plume* which adds an air of authority perhaps, to the opinions being offered or an eye-catching element of the exotic? The Elegant Variation, for example, is suggestive to me of a gold-rimmed spectacled type in a white linen suit, reclining on wicker armchairs in a sun-dappled study crammed to the ceiling with leather-bound volumes gently shaded by giant palms, though it's unlikely that the author measures up to this.

Some bloggers' names are at first glance indicative of the type of blog that you are in for. Ms Baroque in Hackney suggests a perky, fun and modern, if slightly flamboyant type of girl, I think, with a sense of humour and a 'finger on the pulse' of London's cultural history-in-the-making. And indeed she is... A quick glance will reveal that her passion is poetry – there's a list of links to poetry sites and magazines – but she also recommends a selection of 'random books from my library', including French author Michael Houellebecq's *Atomised* at one point, for example, alongside non-fiction works like John Gardiner's *On Moral Fiction*. A recent post saw Ms Baroque praising the virtues of a children's author, in a nice departure from the norm, involving *Babar the Elephant* by Jean de Brunhoff.

Queen Celeste, from *Babar's Travels*

Today's 'Elegantly Dressed' Wednesday post comes to you late – almost too late – in honour of which we bring you a bedtime story... Or not, actually, because to my shame and sadness I have no Babar books here. Otherwise I'd be scanning. And to be honest I am too tired to write much right now. Hence the wishful thinking I can display via this charming picture. The red-piped pyjamas, the tea, the matching brass-tipped beds! It is all one could ask of coziness, and an effortlessly elegant kind of coziness at that. The innate elegance of Babar is contained in, I believe, three elements:

1) A beautiful restrained tone in all the books, in which life is accepted graciously and with a minimum of fuss. This is no small things, as the books are predicated on the early death of Babar's mother, and indeed as he was writing them Jean de Brunhoff was suffering – and then dying – from tuberculosis. But as my great hero Maurice Sendak wrote in his 1981 essay 'Jean de Brunhoff': '[this early loss] permeates all the books, but it is never allowed to overwhelm or destroy Babar's self-confidence. It is living that concerns and delights de Brunhoff. He recognises death as inseparable from the fixed order of things and is never obsessed with it.'

2) Rectitude of bearing and accoutrements; manners; *comme il faut*. This is a lesson that, for example, Jane Austen also teaches us: that life is really much easier and more pleasant if people behave nicely.

3) Sweep of vision; drama, scale, splendour. Sendak writes of children being able to 'climb into' a Babar book (remember, the early ones with script text were enormous), and even with the smaller books we get now the pictures are imposing. The colours are fresh and bright, the composition always wonderful, and the sum always even more than the parts. Sendak further

> says: 'No one before and very few since have utilised the double-spread illustration to such dazzling, dramatic effect. When Babar and Celeste are taken prisoner in *The Travels of Babar*, there is a spectacular circus scene. The handsome red arch that denotes the arena floor is also a menacing symbol of their confinement. There is no doubt that the artist is enjoying himself tremendously... And were the grand parade scene from... [Babar the King] to be set to a joyous march, Berlioz would be most suitable. This picture, by the way, actually moves rhythmically in step if you keep your eye on all those stolid elephant feet, all thumpingly clumping to the same measure. Colour, costume, high comedy mixed with touching solemnity blend into a characteristic composition that appears artless on the surface but is, in fact, extravagantly complex.' Picture now, at the very end, after illness and travail, the small monkey Zephyr carrying a banner which reads: 'Long Live Happiness.'

When Ms Baroque announces on the home page that she is 'a poet, critic, copywriter, editor, conversationalist, style consultant, personal shopper, siren, and housemaid to the gods – at least they think they're gods...' it's clear she has a positive outlook on life and this welcome air of enthusiasm pervades all the postings on her blog.

Bookfox is another sassy sounding young woman whose wit and cunning might just match up to her name. I like, for example, the light hearted sarcasm of posts such as the following comments on Kansas bookshop owner Tom Payne's political protest against the lack of support in the US for the printed word.

> **Posted May 2007**
> A bookstore owner burns books in protest of America's lack of support for the written word. Um, actually, America supports the written word rather well, to the tune of 200,000 new books per year in America alone, so we just can't handle the onslaught of the printed page. Also, depends what books are being burned – I

might have a few more to add to the bonfire.

Or the gentle poking fun at David Mitchell's reading of his new, as yet unnamed, novel at the Hay Festival in 2007:

> **Good news for people who like good news...**
> While *Cloud Atlas* in particular shows his capacity to switch authorial voices, it's hard in a tent in Hay to make the imaginative leap into his new scene: a standoff between exotically named seamen and investigators following up a suspicious fire on board a ship – in 1798 – read out by this boyish-looking Englishman in crew neck and T-shirt.
>
> Mitchell seems to know it, apologising ahead of one character's speech: 'I should be wearing a monocle for this bit.' But it's still a treat. He breaks off occasionally to ask [Peter] Ho Davies of the last paragraph, 'That's got to go, hasn't it?'; or to see if anyone in the audience knows how many guilders the burnt cargo of figurines might actually have been worth in 1798 for historical accuracy: 'I can't find it on the internet or anything.'
>
> No due date for this bouncing baby, but I salivate. I'm in a little bit of a reading slump after finishing *Varieties of Disturbance*, one of those lots to choose from, unable to choose situations. All this David Mitchell news, methinks maybe I should crack one of the two by him I have yet to read – *Number9Dream* or *Black Swan Green*.

For one more example of bloggers who suit their blog names follow Bookfox's link to The Happy Booker. With a pretty smiley cartoon face of a woman, who claims that she is based in the DC area, The Happy Booker 'covers readings and literary events with a smattering of book reviews, author visits, literary interviews and an occasional iPod playlist.'

Writer Wendi Kaufman is the person behind 'the care and feeding of this blog,' and though clearly a busy kind of person

– she is a frequent contributor and reviewer for *The Washington Post*, is currently finishing *Life Above Sea Level,* her first collection of stories and her fiction is doing pretty well (having appeared in *The New Yorker, Fiction, Other Voices, New York Stories*) – she still finds a time and a place in her blog to include a section called 'Read My Friends' Books'. Happy – and generous – indeed.

For some, however, the monikers they select to represent themselves can be misleading. Booksurfer, for example, brings to mind a twenty-something trendy-type offering a superficial dip into a range of lightweight titles. Not so. Martyn Everett's posts on this blog are well-informed, probing and political, with features ranging from a piece on Hans Koning, the Dutch novelist who played a part in the anti-fascist resistance in World War II, or mention of the (yet another) campaign of intimidation that Egyptian writer Nawal El Saadawi is facing for her play *God Resigns at the Summit Meeting* which is charged with disrespecting the principles of Islam, to reviews of less 'intellectual' publications such as detective novels. In fact, Everett ends up arguing that this genre (crime fiction) is far from lightweight – and the review included here just so happens to discuss a book written in 1794…

Reading The Detectives: Escapism or Social Criticism?

What have detective novels got to do with class struggle and revolution? Isn't reading and writing a distraction from the 'real' issues? Does it matter what we read when we sit down and relax after a hard day on the barricades? Aren't all detective novels just another form of bourgeois escapism, with macho heroes defending the political status quo and capitalist property relations?

Of course reading novels can be just another form of escapism and we all need to escape from the pervasiveness of capitalism as it seeps into every aspect of our live, but there can be more to the detective novel than the blood and guts of commercial sensationalism.

In spite of the commercial success of the detective novel in the twentieth century its origins lie in social criticism. The first detective novel, *Caleb Williams*, published in 1794, was written by the anarchist writer William Godwin. Godwin used the account of a murder and its detection by Caleb Williams, a clerk who is the book's hero, to present a radical critique of a despotic society in which the law functioned as just another weapon in the arsenal of the ruling class.

Caleb, is a clerk in the service of Falkland, an aristocrat, when he accidentally discovers that Falkland has committed a murder for which an innocent man was executed. Although Caleb does not intend to reveal his master's crime Falkland has him imprisoned on false charges. Caleb escapes but Falkland relentlessly tracks him down. Eventually, as an act of self-preservation, Caleb tells the truth and Falkland is forced to confess. Even after Falkland's death Caleb Williams is filled with self-reproach and remorse for his own actions, arguing that Falkland had been the product of a corrupt social system, and regretting his own role in the death of the aristocrat.

Caleb Williams contains all the classic elements of the modern detective novel but it is underpinned by a serious indictment of social injustice and a corrupt legal system. The murder and the criminal are both products of the system.'

Of course, some blogging names are simply irritating, such as those varying from the ridiculous or self-consciously nutty like The Mumpsimus (Displaced Thoughts on Misplaced Literatures) or MadInkBeard (this is about comics, admittedly) to the outright unfathomable: has anyone met Bookdwarf (aka Megan Sullivan, one of the frontlist buyers at the Harvard Book Store in Boston)? Or anyone know what the name of online literary magazine *zyzzyva* (www.zyzzyva.org) is meant to refer to?

There are even some which sound distinctly seedy. Take Book/ Daddy, for example, which is suggestive of a pimp, an association of which its creator is well aware (though in fact his wife came up with the name). In a posting from March 2006, Book/Daddy explains how the name came about:

The Book/Daddy name...

...puns on both 'bone daddy' and 'mack daddy.' Think of it as Pimp My Read. 'Bone daddy' is an old slang term for an erection. Stripped of its genital connotations, it was playfully popularized by Tim Burton's *A Nightmare Before Christmas* (1993). 'Mack daddy,' of course, is slang for 'boss pimp,' given worldwide currency by rappers.

My wife Sara came up with 'book daddy' when we switched to DSL service and had to devise a new e-mail address because all possible variations of 'Weeks' and even 'weex' were taken. Such swaggeringly phallic posturing may seem uncharacteristic or just highly improbable for a book columnist. To which I can only note that three women established the well-known litblogs, Bookslut, Bookbitch and Booklust, so a (jokey) masculine handle did not seem out of order.

Besides, Bookninja was already taken. And Pathetic Fallacy would only confuse most readers. Some people have also pointed out that the puns on blues and hiphop slang combined with my name, Jerome Weeks, suggest that I'm black or some white-boy hiphop wannabe: the Eminem of litcrit. Never my intent. I actually did not encounter the African-American association of my name while growing up in Detroit. But after I moved to Texas, many people, black and white, have told me that 'Jerome Weeks' sounds like 'Tyrone Washington' to them. And while working at the *Houston Post* and then *The Dallas Morning News*, I did indeed receive a few calls from readers inquiring about (more accurately, demanding to know) my racial identity.

To which one can only quote Fats Waller: 'One never knows, do one?'

The man behind Book/Daddy, Jerome Weeks, was the books columnist for *The Dallas Morning News* for ten years and its theatre critic for ten years before that. He announces that his site 'ponders print media, literacy, publishing. Anything on wood pulp, pixels or stone is up for discussion,' and he offers some interesting comments on the authority of the critic if you're in the mood for browsing, admitting that he had no relevant qualifications for his post as theatre critic when he took the job but that this didn't necessarily count against him. Book/Daddy quotes Dr Johnson on the site: 'One doesn't have to be a cook to know that the dinner is bad...'

There are some names which just don't sound appealing. Bibliophile Bullpen 'The Whiff of Old Books With Your Coffee' does little for the appetite. Calling yourself Chekhov's Mistress online doesn't exactly set a person up as a barrel of fun and whilst I'm all in favour of keeping it simple, as in the case of he completely unostentatious John Baker's Blog or Kate's Book Blog, some take the simplification to the borders of dull. It's difficult to imagine readers in their thousands rushing for the next instalment of Today in Literature or Reading Experience; though I'm sure there are those who do.

And what about those that blog under a different gender? You might expect a teenage girl to be running Beatrice.com, a literary blog that has been running since 2004, but no – just a click away you will find US male author Ron Howard (*The Stewardess is Flying the Plane*). Actually, we shouldn't poke fun at Howard as, along with Sarah Weinman, he is of course one-half of the husband-and-wife team behind Galley Cat; a hugely successful book blog with an industry edge to it that plays host to parties for the many high flyers of NYC's publishing world. (Although as Ron initially registered the domain name Beatrice.com so that he could sell it back to a food company called Beatrice, we may wonder why he has grown so very fond of it – only joking Ron...!)

That Galley Cat is one of the most popular book blogs in the US, is no doubt because of its coverage of the publishing industry and perhaps also because it is hosted by mediabistro.com which is a website for all bods working within the media, communications and publishing in the US. Here's a quick excerpt from Galley Cat's July 2007 post on the fact that Sebastian Faulks was hired jointly by Penguin UK and Doubleday in the US to write the new James Bond novel – nothing gets past these two, who seem to keep their eyes and ears open to all media-manoueverings, despite the fact that both Ron and Sarah run their own individual book blogs and are no doubt extremely busy (Sarah Weinman is responsible for the mystery blog, Confessions of an Idiosyncratic Mind, which is discussed in the Crime Fiction section shortly). Anyhow, here is the excerpt:

> Score one for MI6, who correctly predicted that Sebastian Faulks, most recently the author of *Engelby*, is the newest author aboard the James Bond enterprise. *Devil May Care* is scheduled to be published on May 28th, 2008 – just in time for the 100th anniversary of Ian Fleming's birth – by Penguin in the UK and Doubleday in the US. Doubleday president and publisher Steve Rubin bought US rights from Gillon Aitken with Deb Futter to edit.
>
> 'Three pages into *Devil May Care* and you are immediately thrown back into the world of James Bond and all those wonderful characters we have come to love,' Rubin said in the announcement, reprinted on Doubleday Broadway's official blog. '*Devil May Care* is pure Fleming channelled by Faulks – a madcap adventure, a romantic romp and a book you can devour in one sitting. It all starts in Paris, and no one alive writes better about Paris than Sebastian Faulks.'
>
> The book will be set in 1967, when, Faulks said yesterday, 'Bond is damaged, ageing and in a sense it is the return of the gun fighter for one last heroic mission'. His own interpretation of the spy, he hinted, would show all the caddishness of Bond's previous incarnations, tempered with just a shade of new-

> mannish sensitivity. He has been widowed and been through a lot of bad things... He is slightly more vulnerable than any previous Bond but at the same time he is both gallant and highly sexed, if you can be both. Although he is a great seducer, he really does appreciate the girls he seduces and he doesn't actually use them badly.'

The best type of name, I think, is chosen when bloggers get more adventurous, adding a touch of glamour perhaps, as with Shaken Not Stirred, the aforementioned The Elegant Variation or Glittering Muse. (Admittedly the latter, which to my mind invokes an image of a foxy-looking 1920s type with spangled-headband, tassled shift dress and cigarette-holder to boot, is in fact rather more concerned with inner-being than book reviewing – the tagline reads: 'Poetic Inspiration, Balanced Living, Humanist Spirituality' – but there are a considerable amount of links to works of poetry, so literary analysis does get a look in.)

Others that are enticing, I think, include phrases directly indicative of personality types. The Inner Minx suggests a saucy blogger, unafraid to voice contentious views, Golden Rule Jones suggests a man of action, who sticks to his principles, someone you can rely on, and LitKicks has a lot to live up to. If you log onto this site late in the day you expect something more uplifting than the cup of tea or sugar rush most people would plump for. And do these people live up to their names? Well, the Inner Minx is a forty-something tom-boyish mother living in Cornwall with a sharp wit and predilection for poetry who clearly relishes the outlet that blogging affords – and according to online club The Shameless Lions Writing Circle she deserves her pseudonym:

> Minx has one of the funniest and sharpest writing blogs in town. She describes slices of her life with genuine wit and charm and takes no prisoners in the process. She has developed a large following with a great mixture of photos, fiction, poems and real

life stories. Minx has written a wonderful book about a witch called Dorcas and is in the process of writing a follow-up. She lives in Cornwall in England with the MD and the Fecker.

My first glimpse of Golden Rule Jones' blog sees him praising one Wall Street Journal writer's 'sensible' approach to the bloggers vs reviews debate and his rapid fire introductions to pieces of news, views and events in the literary sphere certainly don't detract from the image of a practical-minded 'man of action' that his name suggests. In fact, in this lucky plucking of pseudonyms that stand out, all are well-matched. Even Litkicks, with their remit of:

> We don't believe in relaxing with a good book. You can only relax with a mediocre book; a good book can make you so happy you want to scream or so mad you want to kill. This is LitKicks, transmitting words to the world since 1994. Come inside, plug in your brain, and get your minimum daily requirement of Literary Kicks.

OK OK, so if you're not a fan of the beats, existentialism and the jazz age, you may find there is a *slight* bias in favour of this kind of material, but if you are, then kicks will be yours aplenty – and anyhow the focus isn't exclusively in this direction so there's something for everyone. Enjoy!

Ms Snark Literary Agent is another blogger who definitely deserves a mention in any discussion of the web-names people choose. Hers has to be my all time favourite. I don't know if it's the innately bitchy sound of the word 'snark' or the fact that she declares herself 'satan's literary agent' on her personal profile, but there's something about the name that takes my fancy. Setting herself up as a NYC 'consultant' who offers more than the usual literary advice ('How to win and agent and marry George Clooney'), she sends up the publishing industry in a series of 'laugh out loud' posts that have proved popular with everyone from media moguls to papyrophobic wanna-be-authors. Sadly the blog is no longer:

> Where Miss Snark vented her wrath on the hapless world of writers and crushed them to sand beneath her T.Rexual heels of stiletto snark. The blog is dark – no further updates after 5/20/2007.

Which for one fellow NYC based agent is not a moment too soon:

> Dear Miss Snark,
> As a hugely successful and incredibly wealthy New York literary agent, I gotta tell you that you're really causing me heartburn.
>
> In the good old days, crappy writers did a crappy job of submitting their crappy queries, and I was able to cull through the crap at the rate of five per nanosecond, no problemo. And then you came along, dishing up advice and giving away our industry secrets.
>
> I now have thousands of submissions in my slush pile that are perfectly executed, beautifully formatted, and follow my agency's amazingly complex and intentionally contradictory instructions precisely.
>
> So, even though 99.9% of the actual writing is still atrocious, it's taking me ten times longer to slog through the slush.
>
> Are you trying to make my life a living hell, or what?

Other blogs with catchy names include the weblog of New York based poetry fanatic 'Laurable'. As well as pointing out poetry news and publications, her blog has the added feature of listed audio links to poets reading their work which is a nice touch for those of us who can't make it to see them in person.

Rakes Progress is cited as 'a good all-rounder' which 'sifts through the quirkiest things the web has to offer book lovers and does the work for you by picking out the best bits'. A perfectly apt name there then! And Scribbling Woman is suitably diverse, as the name suggests, with an onsite declaration that the blog is 'Probably about books, c18, detritus, parenting, poaching, print, sf, or writing.' Produced by the Assistant Professor of English at the University of New Brunswick, the *Guardian* called this 'a lovely, personal, meandering blog' that is 'thoughtful' and 'insightful'. So perhaps some bookblogs can be judged by their 'covers' ?

Artworks and authors: the nature of the review

But how do these people go about writing reviews? How do they start? Do they improve? Do they continue to enjoy it? How do they avoid being formulaic and/or write engaging, original ideas?

With such close communities forming on the internet between bloggers themselves, but also bloggers and authors, I also wonder to what extent the phenomena of 'small world getting smaller' affects the objectivity, and quality of reviews from bloggers. It may not be easy to write a review when you do not know the artist or individual in question, but it is surely even harder when you do.

Mark Thwaite has a few comments to make about the nature of reviewing, and as the author of two of the best known book blogs in the industry he certainly well-placed to offer advice. As well as writing a blog from the website of online literary journal ReadySteadyBook (see www.readysteadybook.com/Blog.aspx), he also delivers missives from Editor's Corner at The Book Depository where he focuses more on industry related matters. Here's what he has to say about the question of objectivity in terms of how he writes book reviews himself:

> Well, of course, one of the most important things is that ReadySteadyBook is a literary journal, so I give my subjectivity up by passing over the role of reviewing to a number of other contributors. But I review myself too... and the first thing I do is

> 'pre-filter': I tend to know before I read a book whether I'm likely to enjoy it or not.
>
> I'm not going to bother reading some sci-fi, some romance, some chick-lit etc., I'm always going to head for a literary title (or history, philosophy or lit crit) that I'm already likely to enjoy. Then – first rule – I see whether it succeeds on its own terms ie a novel about football doesn't fail because it isn't a novel about rugby! A critic who says 'this book isn't very good because it doesn't mention rugby' has missed the point...

Thwaite is also concerned to emphasise the independence of book bloggers, and how this should place them in a unique position of objectivity:

> One point I want to make very clear is that blogs are way, way more objective than traditional media – bloggers aren't authors. In the newspapers, authors who are friends review each other's books or they review books published by the same publishing house... I hear the blogosphere being condemned – say, for frivolousness, for lack of objectivity, for lack of professionalism – that effects the traditional media just as much if not more...

Andrew Gallix from *3AM Magazine* is another book blogger who is well aware of the freedom that running his own blog entails, to him it consists in the freedom to voice opinions on a book but also choose what to cover in the first place.

> The reason why I launched the very first literary blog (Buzzwords) at *3:AM Magazine* was to concentrate solely on authors and artists I liked: I envisaged it as a good book with all the boring bits left out. So, as a rule, we tend to steer clear of stuff we probably wouldn't like. *3:AM* isn't a public service: we are proud of our preferences and have never attempted to cover all new publications. Unlike many of our more ambitious contemporaries, we are not in the business of

> selling books for publishers – our sole concern is literature.
>
> Even though I am often a little uncomfortable when an obscure writer or a small press get a battering, my policy has always been to ensure that our editors can express themselves freely. Now that we have been going for the best part of a decade, we are increasingly reviewing the works of people we are close to, but that doesn't prevent us from expressing our true feelings. One of our editors, who is also a very talented writer, recently slated a book by Noah Cicero, another very talented Offbeat Generation author we have always supported. Many people in our circles were profoundly shocked by this review, but I stood by it because I feel it is vital to provide a plurality of views and voices. Being published by a small press doesn't place you beyond criticism – not in my book at least.

Gallix is aware that the blogosphere is not without its own problems:

> There is as much nepotism, sycophancy and crass careerism in the blogosphere as in the mainstream press, but lit blogging has had three very positive consequences: it has made literary criticism hip again, it has revived the reputation of authors such as Patrick Hamilton and it has managed to create a buzz around serious contemporary writers like Tom McCarthy.

However, as indicated in the above, he is aware also that as it stands the blogosphere provides a unique environment for the critical appraisal of literature, that should be celebrated as much as protected. Internet reviewing may not be as bias-free as the ideal might suggest, so that evaluation of the reviewers themselves would be a good idea, but such a task is by no means beyond reach. Stay tuned.

Rebecca Gillieron

Bookshop and Booksellers' Blogs

One of the strangest things about being a publisher is that you work in a totally separate environment to the people who really matter in your life – the booksellers. Although we meet a fair number when we have book launches in their shops, we know that it is pretty much a sin to turn up unannounced at a bookshop and actually TALK to a bookseller. They would probably think you were trying to sell them something. They may even be right. So the arrival of the booksellers' blogs means you can get an idea of their concerns, bugbears and personalities in a totally unobtrusive way – by visiting their site and reading their blogs.

It is even nicer when you meet the booksellers in the flesh, we have done one launch with Crockatt & Powell so far, and plan to do more in the future. We have also visited them (by appointment, of course) and seen how they work closely with their customers. When I visited, it was just after tea time. They phone their customers when they know they are on the bus coming home to say the pre-ordered book has arrived, and so the door kept opening and closing as people came in on their way home to pick up their purchases. Matthew Crockatt and Adam Powell seemed to know about the reading habits/love lives/problems of the whole family of the book buyers. It's a bit like *Hollyoaks* but without the drama. Really they should be charging fees for their therapy – they are better than hairdressers for providing a sympathetic ear and the bookshop is a great deal quieter.

Matthew Crockatt and Adam Powell mentioned the success of their previous employee, Marie Phillips, who has landed a very good book deal. Of course, it was a visiting sales representative from the publisher who recommended Marie to their editorial department, so Matthew and Adam feel they should have an agent's fee. No, they are seriously happy for Marie, but miss her in the bookshop. She possibly does not miss the 7am start to the day so the shop can be open for 9am, but judging from her own blog, strugglingauthor.com, she has her own problems too.

Saturday September 30th 2006

See, what I don't understand is why my flat still needs cleaning. I thought this kind of thing didn't happen once all your dreams came true. You mean I still have to take the bins out? What kind of fairytale ending is that?

But I have to admit that when I am not still having to pull handfuls of hair out of the plughole so that my drains don't block – do all published authors have to do this? doesn't it just miraculously disappear from now on? – things have got increasingly exciting. I was invited by my publisher ('my' 'publisher' – can we linger on this a moment?) to a very glamorous party on the night I signed my deal. Martin Amis was launching his new book (called.... um I don't know. I have never read anything by Martin Amis) and there was Will Self, there was Zadie Smith, there was Jung Chang ('Can I introduce you to Jung Chang?' 'Well, only if you want to make my WHOLE LIFE'), there was Kazuo Ishiguru, and there was me. All in the same room. There is something strange about being in a room of famous people, everybody's head looks too big because they are so recognisable that you can't take your eyes off them. It was like being at some kind of literary Disneyland, as if the person next to you is not Kathy Lette but is in fact an unemployed actor wearing a giant plastic Kathy Lette head. (This is true of everyone except Martin Amis, who looks like a miniature scale model of Martin Amis, available from the back of your Sunday supplement for ten easy instalments.) I was still feeling ill and quite intimidated, so I stood in the corner drinking lime squash and wishing I wasn't wearing trainers, while people queued up to tell me how much they loved my book, and every time they did I felt a bit more intimidated, when you would expect it to be the other way around, and also wished even harder that I had been wearing heels, and maybe something other than the H&M trousers with a missing button which are my comfy work slacks for days when I'm not feeling well. (Obviously I was wearing something other than them – I was wearing a T-shirt as well, for a start, but you know what I mean.) I think my favourite comment was from an incredibly friendly, charming woman who enthused that she had been reading my book when she had gastric flu and as soon as she finished it she was 'spectacularly sick.' I can see the advertising campaign right now – Gods Behaving Badly: Read It and Puke. In the end my cold got the better of me and I sneaked away at 10pm wondering if perhaps I am not built for glamour, but maybe with more practise and no temperature and a nice little slinky dress I will be able to hold my own with more confidence.

In the meantime I really need to buy more bin bags and do my laundry. Deas Margaret Atwood vacuum? Does Peter Carey dust? Did Charles Dickens ever panic because he'd run out of bread and it was too late to go to the shops? Questions for the next literary party I think.

PS: I have just done a Google image search for Martin Amis only to discover that the person I took for a miniature scale model of Martin Amis is not only not Martin Amis but doesn't even begin to look like Martin Amis. How I managed to go to Martin Amis's launch party and pick out someone completely at random from the crowd and believe him to be Martin Amis with absolutely no additional evidence to go on is entirely beyond me. I suppose they don't call the publishers 'Random House' for nothing. For the record, the man I picked out had straight floppy hair and glasses and looked like a cross between Penfold from

> Dangermouse and the singer Beck, and was about five feet tall and (now I think of it) only looked about thirty years old (I was suspecting botox). He did look familiar to me; he was probably another famous author. Apologies to Martin Amis, to Penfold, to Beck, and to the small mystery man, whoever he may be.

Adam and Matthew take turns to add to their blog. My overall impression is of two dedicated but irascible individuals, who have surprised themselves by managing to stay afloat in their first year as an independent bookshop. When we did our launch there for Turkish author Elif Shafak, we brought wine and left them the bottles we did not open. They surprised me by saying that independent publishers were far more generous than the giant companies. I am hoping that it's all down to expense accounts and bureaucracy where every penny has to be accounted for. In my years at a very successful children's book publisher, I remember having to explain my receipts to the dragon-like bookkeeper when I returned from my frequent trips to Holland overseeing large board book print runs. 'So, you had a steak, then. And potatoes?' she would bellow. Meekly I would explain that I had three hours to kill on my own that evening before retiring to the rather Spartan hotel room I was staying in – this was before cable TV and the internet. So, it is with pleasure that I can bring to you a few passages from Crockatt & Powell, whose bookshop is in a rapidly gentrifying but rather rough area near Waterloo Station in SE1.

> **The man formally known as...**
>
> Back in the early days we were visited on a regular basis by Flashing Helmet, a man with a hat covered in flashing red lights. Over the year his hat grew more and more battered before finally disappearing over the summer. He claimed it had 'blown away'. Now the nights are drawing in and the wind has a nasty bite. The one formally known as Flashing Helmet has now exchanged his visually distinctive headgear for a brain box cover that appeals (!)

to another sense..smell.

It is a very stinky woolly hat...

September 2nd 2006

We didn't sell our souls at the crossroads

A TV production company offered us £1500 to use our shop to film a candid camera style prank show.

We turned them down.

Our principles are intact even if our bank account isn't.

It still hurts though...

That's a lot of spondoolies...

A lovely moment in an otherwise hot and sweaty day...

A lovely lady wants a ticket for Zadie – but we've sold out. Bummer.

Then she buys two of our lovely Melville press novellas and says we have just become her favourite bookshop.

She lives in New York (bummer) but also said we were better than all the indie shops she knows in New York too!

WOW!

It's SO NICE when we meet people that really GET what we're trying to do.

And now a word from our sponsors

A story from USA Today plops into the Microsoft Outlook Express Inbox on our Compaq laptop. I click on it eagerly with our Logitech wireless mouse. It's about product placement in books...

What I particularly love about product placement in books is the notion that the product will blend seamlessly into the rest of the story, nestling its way unnoticed into the brain of the reader who will have no idea why they suddenly want to buy a Ford. It's bad enough when you see someone drinking a coke in a film, but at least there are a dozen other things on screen your eye could rest on. Product placement in books is the equivalent of zooming right in on the can of coke while the lead actor says, 'I love Coca Cola! It's such a tasty, refreshing beverage! And, by the way, frankly my dear I don't give a damn.'

My absolute favourite example of literary product placement was a book that I once saw which was sponsored by the Gatwick Express. The entire first chapter of the book was devoted to the narrator talking about how brilliant it was shopping in Gatwick airport, so much so that she would go and shop there even when she didn't have a flight to catch.

Of course, people mention brand names in their books all the time, but usually not with one eye on the sales figures. I'm not sure, for example, how sales of Kool-Aid were affected after the release of the *Electric Kool-Aid Acid Test*. (I can make a guess about sales of *Acid*, though.) Where authors mention brands, it's generally to situate the characters in time, place, class – to create context, in other words. It's to aid your suspension of disbelief.

Product placement is the opposite: it's clunky. It stops you short. It makes you forget you were reading about a character and makes you start thinking about toothpaste. Why any author would wish their book to be compromised in this way is a mystery to me. OK, it's not that much of a mystery – it's money of course; but accepting product placement in your novel is a surefire way to make lots of money from advertising and none whatsoever from sales. And I know where I'd rather my cash came from.

...she said, smoothing down the fabric of her Zara skirt and adjusting the straps of her Gap top...

Read this and get angry

Elif Shafak, the Turkish feminist author – and not only one of C&P's biggest sellers, but also an incredibly nice, gracious woman who gave one of the best talks we've ever had here – is the latest in a long line of writers to be put on trial for 'insulting Turkishness'.

It's not even her who's done the insulting – it's a fictional character in one of her novels. But that, it seems, is enough. If convicted, Shafak, who is six months pregnant, faces up to three years in jail.

Saturday December 23rd 2006

Nearly there...Pt 2

This is my last day. Tomorrow, Heathrow permitting, I'm off... Two weeks of total vegetative, monosyllabic relaxation. My poor mother and father will of course attempt to talk to me but I'm afraid the responses may be on the limited side. Marie is off to family in Africa and Matthew is spending three days in Glastonbury on a crazed Cowper Powys quest.

We will go safe in the knowledge that there is enough in the kitty to pay all the bills when we open up again on the 8th January. Hooray.

We set ourselves some targets for December. Yesterday we were just a few pennies short of the point marked 'wildest dreams'. So a big thank you to all down the 'Loo who helped us punch well above our weight. This week we did between a quarter and a fifth of the sales of my previous bookshops at the same time of year (if memory serves) yet we only have less than a tenth of the stock. Our shop mantra of 'Less is More' appears to have paid off. The other shop chant, 'If you build it they will come' also seems to have worked! Of course we do only stock the finest books...

However, 2007 is a whole other story. The twin pitfalls of Hubris and Complacency cannot be allowed to bedevil our minds. Still, if we don't big ourselves up no bugger else will. So once again...

...hooray.

And, *A bientot*.

Another new independent bookshop in England is Mr B's Emporium of Reading Delights in Bath. Nic Bottomley, who runs the shop, used to be a management consultant and tired of spending his life on things he had little interest in. His shop has been going for around a year, and it has several idiosyncracies – a large bath in the middle of the shop floor which is often filled with children's books and toys, a resident small, fluffy dog called Vlaschka who has her very own blog, and a book monkey who gives his opinions on everything, and who writes the blog. We have recently heard that a second independent bookshop has opened in Bath, run by one of the supremos of bookselling, Robert Topping. Will Bath survive the presence of two independent stalwarts? Can I cope with my own divided loyalties? I hope there are plenty of book buyers in Bath who will support both shops and that they are here to stay.

Nic Bottomley is extremely open to independent publishers contacting him with ideas for launches and promotions. He is not a little critical of large publishers who find a rather vapid idea and then flog it to death, even if it does bring him income. He is also very honest about the downs of bookselling – the report from a day in his first week when he sold one book all day is telling.

November 29th 2006 at noon

The Book Monkey's *Dangerous Book for Monkeys*

I have a fantastic new idea for a book – but keep it hush for now. Between you and me, I reckon I'll make a fortune out of a spin-off Monkey version of the wildly popular *Dangerous Book for Boys*.

In case you've been asleep for the past few months, or chained to your desks or, like me, been working like a (well, I would say dog but...)...anyway, if for some reason you've been out of the loop, this book is a fabulous giftbook detailing all sorts of things that boys used to do in the days before the onslaught of virtual 'Beat-the-Living-***Out-of-Someone-From-the-Comfort-Of-Your-Bedroom' games. It's full of things like 'how to make a go-cart' or a water bomb, cricket rules, famous battles, how to juggle, extraordinary adventurers...that kind of thing.

However, I reckon it's mostly a winner because no-one knows

what to buy boys or men and this title just screams 'BUY ME – I'M PERFECT FOR ANY MAN'.

My monkey version would also be very practical and full of lists – how to peel fruit without the mess, the complete words to 'King of the Swingers', fifty ways to tease a Ring Master, origami with banana leaves, opening crisp packets, lists of all Tarzan films...etc...

I am sure my proposal will be a huge hit for the following reasons:

(1) Monkeys love lists too
(2) People never know what to buy monkeys
(3) It is bound to make Richard & Judy's list thus making me an instant millionaire. They are suckers for this kind of thing.

So... watch this space, monkey-lovers...

Practising my Sudoku – posted October 23rd 2006 at 8pm – Heathrow

So, Mr Thundermug eluded me, but some sympathy I got from Mr B! I was expecting to return home to a nice bowl of Coco Pops and a bit of TLC but instead was ordered to go straight back off to find the new country of the month books and films – in Japan no less! If I didn't have such a thick hide, I'd think Mr B was trying to keep me out of the way while all these great events are going on.

Still, I am partial to Sushi, gadgets and to having my photo taken so I reckon I'll love it there. Have already got into Sudoku in preparation for the long flight. In any case, I'm so glad I missed the Afternoon Tea with the Llewelyn-Bowens. He doesn't strike me as the monkey-loving type, what with the floaty sleeves and design talk. It seems that in any case he was all over Vlashka and I'm not sure I could have stomached that love-up.

So see you, monkey-fans. I will return with long armfuls of Murakami and much much more very soon!

Gone in search of Mr Thundermug – posted October 5th 2006 at 2pm

Am downhearted today. After reading Mr Thundermug, I have become unable to sleep, eat, let alone work until I find this god, this hero, this talking monkey *extraordinaire*. I thought featuring him as in the book of the week would satisfy me, but no. I've been Thundermugged. And I'm not alone. Everyone's talking about him. Every blogger in the land seems to be caught under his spell. So I'm off. So long Mr B, for now at least. You've worked me like a PG Tips chimp for long enough. I'm coming Mr Thundermug. Wherever you may be. I'm on my way.

Homer sweet Homer – posted August 11th 2006 at 4pm

Did you ever see that episode of *The Simpsons* where they find out that the monkey sanctuary is really a diamond mine using monkeys as free labour? Well I know how those mining monkeys feel. Mr B has had me working like a dog for the last few weeks, hence my lack of blogging. Come to think of it, where do they get that 'working like a dog' phrase from? As I type, Mr B's dog is flaked out in the usual heap of fur doing nothing remotely work-like.

Meanwhile I've been off to sodding Canada to report back on their best literary offerings for this damn 'country of the month' feature. And no, a free month's holiday to Canada may not sound bad to you, but then you probably wouldn't have to fly over in a wire cage with a tarpaulin over it would you? And I suspect you'd choose to spend the first three weeks of your trip in Banff or Vancouver Island or some such, whereas monkey-boy here was obliged to spend it in a concrete hut in Toronto airport listening to the vet's Celine Dion CDs on loop and having inoculation needles shoved in him every five minutes.

So it was good to get home and, surprise of surprises, when I checked my inbox I had my very own email. My first, I must confess. It was from a rather fabulous if slightly ambitious fellow by the name of Comandante Monkey who is one of the all-too-small community of monkey bloggers. His revolutionary blog is online too and he was kind enough to point his readers to this page. So I'll repay the compliment.

King Kong – posted July 3rd 2006 at 5pm
Second week of trading. Rainy Monday. Whole country depressed after England getting knocked out of the world cup – you do the maths. Not a customer in sight.

So, apart from when Mr B called for a sales update ('No sir, not one thousand. One book') I've spent my day watching *King-Kong* – the original of course, not this new-fangled rubbish. Man that's one big monkey.

The Bookshop at Crow on the Hill is run by Jonathan Main and Justine Crow who is a frequent comment leaver on Scott Pack's blog. His shop is in far distant Crystal Palace so I have not visited, but his entries on ninety-nine ways to ask for a book struck a chord. I could match it with ways people have tried to sell their manuscripts to us, the emotional blackmail, the wrenching of hearts, the intellectual name dropping. However, Crow's punters are there in the flesh before him, and so their foibles are so much more immediate:

April 2nd 2007
My friend says I would like *The Observations* by Jane Harris the slightly imperious lady says. Adding, have you read it?

No, sorry I haven't, I say.

There's a copy in the window, do you have one in the shop?

I retrieve a copy from new titles.

The lady reads the back cover. Oh God, Scotland in 1863. No thank you. No.

What can you recommend me?

What sort of thing do you normally read? I ask.

Saramago, she says. I'm very keen on Saramago.

Game on, I think.

I scan two bays of new titles; a small expanse of something like a hundred books. There is nothing remotely Saramago-like amongst them.

Standards, I think, must be slipping.

Beckett, the lady says, picking up a copy of *Beckett Remembering: Remembering Beckett*. You can't go wrong with Beckett.

No, I say, indeed, you can't.

Phew.

February 14th 2007

Book arrives at 1.31pm. Text customer having unpacked the box and printed out the 'slips' (technical term). Customer collects book at 2.29pm.

Thanks, you've really saved the day.

No problem, say I, whilst checking to see if I am wearing my underpants outside my trousers.

Then, as if to confirm my superhero status, the very next customer buys a copy of *New Kobbe's Opera Book*, for fifty whole English pounds (yes!).

February 13th 2007

Which one were you looking for?

Purgatory. It's *Prison Diaries* Volume 2. Only I ordered it from Woolworths two weeks ago but they still haven't delivered it and I need it for tomorrow.

February 6th 2007

'I like to order my books from you,' the man said, handling his latest order of a volume of pretty obscure Japanese Art, because you see the V&A and the British Library don't take Book Tokens, and you take Book Tokens don't you.'

'Yes we still do,' (reluctantly) I said.

'That's good.' He looked at the book some more. 'I was just reading a review of this, this morning,' he said. 'Of course I know the chap who did the review, he used to be our man in Tokyo...Anyway how much is it?'

'£16.99,' I said.

'Good,' he said and rooting in his wallet, handed me £15.00 worth of Marks and Spencer's vouchers and a two pound coin.

February 1st 2007

A lady is banging on the door.

I'm ten minutes late opening. I greet her with my best smile. 'Books for a three year old?' she asks, hovering around the children's picture flats.

'Boy or girl?' I ask, attempting to turn on the computer and put the float in the till.

'Girl.'

'Well, the one you have in your hand – *Commotion in the Ocean*, by Giles Andreae – would be fine,' I say.

'I need two.'

'Okay, well this one is very good too,' I say, picking up a copy of *Wolves* by Emily Gravett.

'That's fine. I need an envelope to post them in. Any kind of envelope will do. I need to get them off straight away.'

I pick up a large white padded envelope that I have just emptied a HarperCollins proof out of, and show her that the books fit perfectly.

'Don't you have an ordinary brown one?'

'No sorry, this is all I have.' I ring up the books.

'How much is that?'

'£10.98.'

'HOW MUCH!?'

'£10.98.'

'But we only spend £5.00 on our children... I'll just take that one.'

'That's £5.99 then. Thanks.'

She hands me £5.10. 'And I don't want the envelope!'

Luckily, I was late because I had been 'doing' yoga.

So, there's one in the eye for those who think bookselling is a stress free occupation.

'Bookseller to the Stars' Mark Farley

Crockatt & Powell are not the only independent booksellers who the public see as a kind of universal supplier. It is hard to think of assistants in WH Smith or Waterstone's being asked similar questions, although as I have not asked booksellers in these shops I may be wrong. Certainly, as publishers, we are asked to provide all kinds of recommendations (highest on the list is, can we recommend literary agents or publishers for a proposal we have tactfully declined – as the publishing industry is small, it is always hard to knowingly subject a colleague to a task which they will not appreciate being given). But here is the account of Bookseller to the Stars, Mark Farley, on his role as optician:

Saturday April 8th 2006

Reading glasses now on sale... Sorta

Yes, we have reading glasses on sale.

No, this does not mean that we either:

a) fix them

b) give eye tests

c) know the number of the best opticians that will suit you.

I say we sell reading glasses but in reality people just steal them.

Case in point:

'Excuse me, there are no glasses in this case...'

The glasses come in very this cylindrical cases, easy to palm with your basic street magician training and have the usual addition of not being security tagged.

'Yeah, somebody probably took them...'

'What do you mean took them?'

Took them, thieved, half-inched, twocked, swiped, stolen, took them...'

'Oh, what... around here?'

'Yeah, especially around here...'

Really, some people live in a bubble...

What people really want, it seems, are the kind of shops that only appear these days in soap operas – leaning shelves full of everything someone could possibly want with a shopkeeper who has all day. We do ourselves sell books from the office, and occasionally people ring the doorbell and come in to browse our shelves. As we sit trying to work at our computers, I have to remind myself that bookshops are open to all, and provide a lovely environment in which to read books that people have no intention of buying. People stay for over an hour, asking us the odd question. We are, of course, charming. No wonder we all like communicating remotely via the internet.

Catheryn Kilgarriff

Publishers' Blogs

There are two blogs which are turned to frequently in this office, because the writers always have something to say, and because they are both fairly new independent publishers. These are the blogs of Scott Pack, the Commercial Director (I am not sure this job description exists anywhere else in publishing) of The Friday Project and Emma Barnes of Snowbooks. Both put considerably more effort into their blogs than we do – although I sometimes wonder if that is because life is easier for them, as the chains have all ordered thousands of their books, or because they do more blogging than editing. Or something. Emma seems to work all the time, poor love and I often feel sorry for her. I hope that soon she will manage to get out more and enjoy being thirty-something.

Emma's is the more useful blog to us since she goes into details on the nitty gritty of computer systems and the power of using various programmes. We have usually found simple ways of doing what she does already but we have Macs so our software is different in any case. Her posting of pictures of the Snowbooks *Richard & Judy* submission was helpful as we could see that going the extra mile just may help. So much for independent publishing being a live version of *Black Books*: we should all aspire to being glossy and polished. When she posts about having a negative sales figure in March because of returns from October, though, I do want to shout loudly that it doesn't have to be that way – it's due to how your distributor pays you (a certain percentage each month, spread out over five months, means that returns from five months ago can still be hurting you.). It's possible for distributors to use returns in such a way that you never get paid – we had a similar situation in the US around seven years ago. Thankfully, this distributor is not in business and we had moved and successfully got our last dollars out of them before the grim reaper struck.

So it's really a silent community that supports one another. When Emma posts that she has spent several days placing photos in Photoshop for one of her boxing books, I am happy when I read somewhere that there are over 500,000 people doing martial arts in England. I hope they are all buying her books.

Scott has esoteric book tastes and this is what made him so valuable to an independent publisher like us when he was Head Buyer at Waterstone's. I think I have only met him once and I would quake before picking up the telephone to him – I think I did it twice in four years – but I was always rewarded with a sizeable order for books which were attracting attention in the media. His cover design advice I found hard to swallow, but I did, and now I think it makes sense. Scott's view is that authors and publishers are well-served to make their books look like they have come from a large publishing house, even if this means they sport generic photographs with large display type. But then I earned my living in a large design consultancy for many years and have seen the power of the new. Recently, Scott has mentioned medical problems and spent a lot of time working from home, so if he stops blogging I start worrying. But then he starts to write about the talks he has been giving, so I realise that fear of flying/lack of passport or whatever reason he didn't make it to the Frankfurt Book Fair is probably a smoke screen for having better things to do.

Scott and Emma's blogs frequently refer to each other's businesses, and they comment a great deal on the other's site. It's a kind of active virtual friendship, which is nice to see. I cannot imagine the editorial departments of the large houses keeping up such a constant and public dialogue. Here are a couple of extracts:

Firstly, a typical Snowbooks blog, detailing what she should be doing. I have lists like this everywhere in this office (on the computer screen, in my notebook, on the wall) but I still like reading someone else's:

October 26th 2006: If I was a good person...

...this is what I would have achieved. Welcome, friends, to a section of my To Do list:

• Figure out way to get AIs and reading copies to all retailers electronically (save postage, save time, save trees) in a form that's easy for them to read

• Learn advanced XML: crucial for a publisher who wants to sort out her content management

• Learn Java

• Schedule printing for 2008; consolidate schedule where possible to save money

• Figure out new way to upload images etc to various partners' FTP sites automatically

• Revisit e-book terms

• Finish all ERRPs (Emergency Reprint Readiness Packs, of course. We like to amend our files as soon as we see an error, which can happen, so that the reprint is error free. Plus we like stupid acronyms)

• Analysis of total cost of distribution. Contract says x%; last time I did this analysis it was x+5%.

• Learn SQL

• Revise online selling strategy

• Create PR packs, in case one of our books flies, or we're in the papers and need a bunch of beautifully-formatted info about the company STAT

• Update list of prizes suitable for our books and enter them

• Photoshop 1280 photos (next year's martial arts books). Each photo takes about twenty mins.

• Find better way to Photoshop things.

- Edit everything that needs editing
- Scan all contracts and archive (there's one task that will never get done)
- Run payroll
- Pay bills
- Bookkeeping
- Fix thing
- Do other thing
- Write to that person about that thing [trails off...]

And here is Emma on books she thinks affected her, for possibly the wrong reason:

February 4th 2007 9:14 am

I've just emailed Scott Pack to ask for the name of his chippie that he recommended because our shelves in our spare bedroom at home are so over-stocked that they're hanging off the wall at a very odd angle, ready to fall off and smash into bits any moment now. They're practically defying gravity, when you look at them. I always tread very carefully when I go in. And no, I didn't finish *In Search of Lost Time.* And creeping about under them reminds me of a time when I was grubbing around under a shelf, stood up too quickly and knocked the *Reader's Digest Book of DIY* off its perch, which fell on my head and cut it open. I still have the scar and a sore patch, five years later. It got me thinking: what other books have led to pain and misery? Here are my top five.

1) *Reader's Digest DIY book*, as above.

2) Jane Austen's *Emma.* I couldn't stop reading it when I was meant to be revising for my mock A levels. I did very badly as a result, and didn't realise that those results would be used as my forecast grades for my UCCA form. Cue a lot of hard work and begging and heartache that could have been avoided.

3) *The Good News Bible.* I was given one when I got confirmed

when I was fourteen or so, and read it – twice. It made absolutely no sense to me at all. I really wanted to believe in God because I thought I would burn in a fiery fireball of fire for all eternity if I didn't, but the Bible gave me nothing to believe in. I genuinely went through a lot of anguish until I started my history A level, put it all in context, and formed my current atheistic view of religion. It makes me very, er, cross that the church should put a child through that, at the same time as all those hormones and hard academic work.

4) Martin Amis's *London Fields*. It thoroughly depressed me and touched a nerve as at the time I was feeling very anti-London. For weeks afterwards everywhere I went I saw blackness and dirt and cruelty in people and sordidity. Maybe that makes it a good book, in that it stays with you, but I wished it would leave me alone.

5) *Retail Therapy* by Rob Jones. This is an all-ends-well story because it resulted in the formation of Snowbooks, which I'm obviously very happy about – but at the time it was very sad. Rob got a publishing deal (with a very unimpressive advance) for this book, which he spent a good six months writing. It is a seminal work, in terms of both content and style, and could easily have been a crossover mass market success. However, the experience with the publisher was ghastly. They put it out as a hardback, gave it a bland cover, and tried hard to shoe-horn it into their useless series brand. I remember Rob telling me what happened in an editorial meeting. The editor was flicking through the manuscript and said 'Could you just put in, you know, a few more graphs?' Rob readily agreed, being an affable type, and asked which points the editor felt required support. 'Oh, nothing in particular – we would just like to see a few more pictures.' Pity the poor reader of that series. Rob's experience – and, as I'm his best pal, my experience too – was so rotten and demeaning and saddening that we thought we could easily do better. And we do! How's about that then.

So those are mine. What about yours? We might have to do books of pleasure soon, to counter all this misery!

Let's hope that the last book which led to the starting of Snowbooks is not something they regret – I'm sure it isn't. I wonder who the publisher was though.

Scott Pack's shelves are a work of art and you will just have to go to his blog to find the photographs of them since this is not an illustrated book. Now that would be really silly, reproducing in expensive coated paper images which you can hopefully still find on the internet. His level and depth of reading is extremely impressive and I almost do not dare choose one extract from his blog, since it seems to touch on everything and everybody, but here goes. This is his entry on short stories. It would be wonderful if short stories did suddenly become popular and commercially viable. I was kept sane by *Granta* magazine in the dark years of having two children under four when the most time I had to myself for reading was just long enough for a few of the excellent *Granta* extracts – all beautifully chosen and presented to you in a volume of related stories from different authors. *Granta* still takes up over two shelves in our house and we are still adding to it as subscribers. Blogs do have a power to bring attention to underrated creative art forms and Scott is bang on about short stories. His phrase 'Great to read, buggers to sell' was picked up by several news stories about the format as this blog came out around the time of the results of the second National Short Story competition, which had over 400 entries.

April 24th 2007

Short stories: great to read, buggers to sell.

I love them myself. I always have at least one collection on the go and find them wonderful to dip into when I have a few spare moments, or last thing before shut eye.

They are a real pig to publish though. The market is tiny. It is rare for a collection to sell very much at all. People claim to read stories but so few actually shell out for a book of them. I can bloody talk, for the past six years I have been given most of my books for free. 90% of my short story books didn't cost me anything so it isn't surprising that I am prepared to give them a go. I'd like to think I'd own almost as many if I had to pay for them but, let's be honest, I wouldn't.

UK publishers and writers often peer enviously over the pond to America where the short story seems to be a popular and commercial art form. My friends in the trade over there tell me that isn't the case at all but it bloody well looks like it to me – hundreds of literary magazines, collections in the bestseller lists, anthologies of the finest stories every year. That compares more than favourably thank you very much.

Naturally there are exceptions and the UK charts will occasionally be dented by a new collection or the like, but the prevailing wind rarely puffs up the sales (sorry) of the short story. As a result, publishers will go out of their way to hide the fact that a book is a story collection at all – look at Matthew Kneale's *Small Crimes in the age of Abundance*, cunningly disguised as a novel. And some of our finest novelists – David Mitchell and Dan Rhodes for example – are really short story writers who have become adept at linking their tales together to create the longer form.

There are occasional attempts to kick start interest in short stories – the current Radio 4/*Prospect* competition is very welcome (if seemingly for big name authors only), and we shouldn't ignore the indie scene – magazines, both printed and online – which beavers away valiantly. But they don't seem to make a lasting difference to what is a pretty dormant market.

I have a few ideas that could, perhaps, help to grow the readership of stories in this country but they need a lot more thought and a hefty amount of collaboration so I will shut up about them for now and make more noise once I've sounded out a few interested parties.

Anyway, this whole preamble is leading up to a book review

which concerns, naturally enough, a collection of stories. *Leading The Dance* is the debut collection from a friend of Big Mouth, Sarah Salway. As mentioned above, I tend to dip into story collections and they consequently take me some time to get through (Richard Yates' *Collected Stories* has been on the go for six months now) but this was a book I couldn't resist reading from start to finish. Having completed one story I was eager to move on to the next, pausing merely for a cup of tea or quick browse of the internet as a form of punctuation...

'All killers no fillers' refers to an album where every track is a corker. The pop world was notorious for padding out albums with sub-standard songs, surrounding a couple of hit singles with fillers and hoping for the best, and we've all got CDs in our collections which would have to plead guilty to that crime. I often find that story collections try the same trick – two or three stunning pieces alongside less impressive fodder – but that is most certainly not the case here. *Leading The Dance* is as fine a collection as you are likely to read. Eighteen beautifully crafted stories, several of which will linger long in the memory. Like *Quiet Hour*, in which a small boy is left to play in his father's new car while his parents go upstairs 'for a sleep' with predictably unpleasant results. Or *Blind*, where a cleaner working for a blind man strips naked while she dusts and hoovers to see if he'd notice. And my favourite, *Painting The Family Pet*, which sees a troubled suburban housewife employ a pet portrait painter even though there are no animals in the house.

There are twists in some, others are revealing slices of life. All are incredibly well-observed and full of the meaningless minutiae of human existence which become so meaningful when Salway gets her hands on them. I would heartily recommend anything she has written but this would be a fine place to start.

Scott Pack was known as the most powerful bookseller buyer when he was at Waterstone's Head Office for six years, and what is undoubtedly true is that he was a great supporter of independent publishing. Now, as an independent publisher himself, he is finding many of the same obstacles we have been up against for years. He has recently had four books featured on *Richard & Judy* and found it difficult to get the books promoted in the chains, so the sales have migrated online. Thankfully, online is an alternative, although it would be hard to imagine a major publishing house having similar problems and having to console itself with Amazon figures. His blog is read by many people in the book trade and is a brilliant showcase for issues in the trade.

Catheryn Kilgarriff

Fan Blogs, Obsessives and the Extreme

Though even the most modest book bloggers may occasionally exhibit a tendency to write their mornings away, detailing every cup of coffee to their first flick through the papers, there are those that are so completely obsessed with their subject matter that there is no room left on their websites to mention their own lives in any shape or form. Cue sighs of relief.

Take the book bloggers whose posts are like fan blogs, focusing on one particular author or genre, with no desire to stray beyond their chosen sources of joy, which can apparently provide endless food for thought, pure entertainment and delight in equal measure and seemingly without end. Where do these people get their inspiration, years after an author is dead and gone and with no new works appearing? You'd be surprised...

Brontë Blog

'But let me think that if today it pines in cold captivity;
To-morrow shall soon be away, eternally, entirely Free.'

As the name suggests, The Brontë Blog spot features all things Emily-Anne-and-Charlotte related – everything from quotes from the Brontës' husbands to reviews of discussion groups held by Brontë fanatics and biographers, analysis of texts from Brontë fans and wannabe writers who hope to continue 'writing-in-the-style-of'. There is an impressive selection of Brontë 'e-texts' that the reader can choose from including the works of the sisters themselves – yes, *Jane Eyre* in its entirety! – as well as a number of non-fiction works on the Brontës themselves. The 'Useful Links' section can hook you up with organisations like The Brussels Brontë Group, the links to other Brontë bloggers can put you in touch with Agnes Grey, Brontë Society, Brontëana, the Brontëites and even Emily Brontë or Charlotte Brontë. Not forgetting Reverend Patrick Brontë, their father. You can even vote for your favourite Brontë Parsonage from the UK or add your name to the list of supporters for a Campaign to Erect a Blue Plaque for George Smith at the publisher's residence…and no, I didn't know he was a one-time Brontë publisher either until I visited this site, but I do now!

It would be difficult to imagine anything more wholeheartedly thorough. Ms Brontë Blog is 100% dedicated to the cause and with a suitably 18th century violent passion that she expects everyone else to share (see the call for voluntary proof readers for the complete e-texts of the Brontës' works that she has posted online for all to enjoy). This woman lives, breathes and sees the Brontës every step of the way. Remember the avowals of devotion from the heroine in *Wuthering Heights* 'Nelly, I am Heathcliff!'? Well, it's not hard to picture a similar 'Readers, I AM the Brontës!' Full marks for dedication.

Here's a selection of the posts listed June 2007 which demonstrate the variety of material and contributions featured on the site:

A laidback Heathcliff, Bertha Rochester and *The Sopranos*

More reviews for the York Theatre Royal's production of *Wuthering Heights*. *The Times* gives three stars out of five:

> 'Jane Thornton's deft, economical adaptation of Emily Brontë's classic novel remains a period piece. And yet a case could

almost be made for Sue Dunderdale's pacey production of it to be seen and studied by anyone interested in the psychology of contemporary adolescents. After all, aren't young people today just as temperamental, conflicted in their emotions and wilful in their decisions as those depicted by Brontë in the mid-19th century?...

...Dunderdale puts a talented young cast of five through some vigorous paces. The actors play their parts and further the plot as narrators, slipping between multiple duties with relative simplicity and assurance. Lorna Ritchie's attractive split-level set allows them plenty of room to manoeuvre. With its hard, horizontal lines offset by a double staircase, it functions almost like a playground upon which they enact a complicated, sober game of let's pretend.

Perhaps inevitably, given the small size of the cast, some muddiness arises in the second act as Brontë's tangled, troubled tale tumbles into the next generation. A family tree might have come in handy just to keep track of who begat whom.

That's not all that's missing here. Harris makes a fine Cathy. You believe that this spirited and, frankly, selfish girl would die for love. Fry's slouching, laid-back Heathcliff is no match for her. He's uncouth and sulky but not, as described in the script, fierce and wolfish. The actor simply hasn't enough strength of presence to help lift the show to the higher levels of feeling to which it aspires.' (Donald Hutera)

Talking about theatrical adaptations of Brontë novels, Imogen Russell Williams posts on the *Guardian*'s Theatre Blog about transferring popular novels to the stage and describes Polly Teale's *Jane Eyre* like this:

There have been some outstanding adaptations of books for the stage. Polly Teale's brilliant version of *Jane Eyre,* which envisaged Bertha Rochester as Jane's dangerous, sensual alter ego, is one.

Bertha also appears on *The Minnesota Women's Press* that unveils another interesting Brontë reference. This is an article about lesbian writer's communities in Minnesota:

> But three writers we spoke with are members of a local writing group called Bertha, which began in the 1980s. Writer Morgan Grayce Willow, whose poetry has been published in journals and anthologies, explained, 'It's named for Bertha Rochester, the "Madwoman in the Attic" referred to in the seminal feminist critical work of the same name... Bertha Rochester being, of course, the mad wife of Rochester in *Jane Eyre* by Charlotte Brontë. Hers is the dark tale that's hidden, yet nurtured, which eventually, inevitably surfaces as it must.' (Nancy Hedin)

The three writers, new Brontëites to be added to our ever-growing list, are Morgan Grayce Willow, Barrie Jean Borich and Judith Katz.

We read on the *Clackamas Review* how the new Memory Garden of the Oregon City High School contains an unexpected Brontë reference:

An engraved plaque recalls the words of Charlotte Brontë:

> 'There's no use in weeping, Though we are condemned to part: There's such a thing as keeping a remembrance in one's heart...' (Patrick Sherman).

The words belong to her poem 'Parting'.

On the blogosphere today: the Brontë Parsonage Blog gives you the chance to know the youngest member of the Brontë Society, and arguably the cutest, Rachel Angela just eight weeks old.

> Angelic Teacher visits Haworth and posts about it (no pictures, though). Poet Silvia Palferro devotes a poem to Emily Brontë: '*Tejido Salvaje*' (in Spanish)...A long article in Portuguese devoted to Paula Rego (with special mention to her *Wide Sargasso Sea* works). A review of *Jane Eyre* in Italian published on CastleRock. And, finally, this puzzling comment on Dystel & Goderich Literary Management blog:
>
> > On the other hand, I'm happy enough to obsess about the greatness of a groundbreaking television series (*The Sopranos*) and the parallels between the last episode's shocking sign-off and Charlotte Brontë's brilliant and mostly overlooked *Villette* (any of you agree?) and not at all embarrassed to discuss it.
> >
> > We haven't seen the episode...but if anybody can enlighten us, please do it.

It would be difficult to find a fan site that is more dedicated to its literary heroes – or in this case literary heroines – than this one. However, there are a number of blogs that might consider themselves contenders.

Elementary my dear bloggers!

One fictional character who certainly inspires devotion to the point of obsession is 'national treasure' Sherlock Holmes. So few would want to claim that Conan Doyle is a 'literary great' but his character is certainly a favourite, and the sheer array of bloggers writing about Holmes is testament to this. Opening with a suitably Holmes-ish invitation to join in –'The game's afoot as Scott Monty blogs about the world of Sherlock Holmes. Quick, Watson! Subscribe!' – The Baker Street Blog is for all fans of the pipe-smoking, deerstalker-hat-wearing great-British-detective. Don't sign-up unless you're willing to take it all in the right spirit, however, as this really is a light-hearted celebration of all that is faintly ridiculous and 'jolly-good-fun' in the world of Watston and Holmes.

There are links to podcasts (with interviews, Holmes history, story-telling and discussions, titled 'I Hear of Sherlock'), listings about Holmes-related events both in the US and the UK. But not to be outdone in terms of Sherlock trivia, fans of Conan Doyle are also blessed with A Study In Sherlock, another in-depth Holmes fansite. With the opening quotes 'It is a capital mistake to theorise before one has data,' taken from the book *A Scandal in Bohemia,* links to Holmes comics, trinkets, rare books and antiques, audio clips, graphics and other paraphernalia, alongside 'eye-catching' headlines on the home page linking to the full-story such as:

> 06/08/01 – The English added fish and chips, Sherlock Holmes and the Oxford English Dictionary to its list of national treasures ...along with *Monty Python*, Robin Hood, the Mini and the long-running BBC Radio 4 soap opera *The Archers*...

You can also join mailing lists like 'Hounds of the Internet' or join the 'Dr. Watson's Neglected Patients' Society' should the mood take you. And if you think this is all going a bit too far, you've seen nothing yet. Just a click or two away a whole world of Sherlock Holmes spoofs awaits. (See Solar Pons.)

Blogging by character

It must be extremely satisfying for an author to create characters so striking that readers become a fan of the creation rather than the creator. How many people could describe Lolita but fail to recognise Nabakov? How many know the story of Alice in Wonderland and how many could name Lewis Caroll?

Ian Fleming is sadly no longer around to enjoy the surge in popularity actor Daniel Craig has secured for his Bond character, but the recent film of his first novel *Casino Royale* has been good news for the many fan blogs that have established a presence on the net. For example, the James Bond 007 blog has a nice look to it, the simple layout and retro colours and fonts are easy on the eye and I like the daily round-up of 'Bond headlines from around the world'. With a simple click you can whisk yourself off to read 'Melville: The Man Behind M' in the *Irish Post*, or 'Penguin Planning a Celebration of 007 in 2008' on CommanderBond.net.

Actually, CommanderBond.net is itself a must-read if you happen to have a penchant for Bond blogs. With sections on *Casino Royale* and the forthcoming *Bond 22*, it's bang up to date, in-your-face and chock-full of Bond gossip from across the globe, as well as competitions, forums, podcasts and a link to S-branch.net – an incredibly in-depth archive of information on Bond books, films, music, Bond girls (and when I say in-depth I mean it, for each film there is production information, plot synopsis, cast lists, crew lists, gadgets, quotes, release history, trivia, taglines, box-office information, premieres, awards, foreign title translations, CBN articles, and a whole lot more besides...happy reading?)

But we stray from the stuff of literary fiction! Which is perhaps forgivable when fan blogs in this genre aren't always so easy to spot. Take The Master and the Margareader for example, which is labelled as 'A bookclub. A drinking society. *Erleichda,*' though it's scope is hardly limited to Mikhail Bulgakov's work. With contributions from seven different bloggers including 'Antigone' and 'Damian' you'd expect the content to be dark, but whilst posts include a review of Nick Cave's *The Ass and the Angel*, there are also recommendations for lighter reads such as *Sunday Times* bestseller *The Yes Man* by Danny Wallace – whom UK TV presenter Davina McCall calls 'a genius'. Elsewhere you might think that A Grimm Perspective was a Hans Christian Anderson blog – not so! – and if you think Heathcliff.stumbleupon.com will zip you straight to star-struck musings on a 'pitiless wolfish man' roaming the Yorkshire moors you are sadly mistaken. Misleading monikers will not take you to the destination you require in this instance either (this 'Heathcliff' is a sociable sounding eighteen year old in Alwaye, KL, India and not a whiff of literature in sight. In fact under his 'wanted' poster is the tagline: 'Those who think it's cool not to touch a book and never read.')

No discussion of literary fan blogs that focus on a particular character would be complete without a quick mention of the Harry Potter phenomenon. JK Rowling 'herself' is not averse to the odd posting (or some PR assistant of hers anyway). On the official website there is a fancy home page with details of her latest author tours and postings about things like the Harry Potter books being included on the year's 'most banned books' (after all, 'No publicity is bad publicity!' etc.). 'Rowling' writes:

> **September 29th 2006**
> Once again, the Harry Potter books feature on this year's list of most banned books. Once again I take my annual inclusion on the list as a great honour. As it puts me in the company of Harper Lee, Mark Twain, JD Salinger, William Golding, John Steinbeck and other writers I revere, I have always taken my inclusion on the list as a great honour. 'Every burned book enlightens the world.' (Ralph Waldo Emerson)

It's not clear where Rowling feels she gets the authority to place herself alongside the likes of Steinbeck or Golding with her tales of flying broomsticks and magic balls, but the sentiment is admirable. I only really mention Rowling's postings as an excuse to cover 'Leaky', The Leaky Cauldron Harry Potter fansite, run by Melissa Anelli, John Noe and Sue Upton. With news, features, video clips, essays, a chatroom, 'Pottercast' podcast, and interviews with Rowling herself, it probably deserves its name as the best Potter fansite on the web – with apologies to Mugglenet, its close rival, by all accounts (along with the less interestingly-named Harry Potter Fan Zone). In fact Rowling awarded Leaky her 'Best Fan Site' award. For those of you who definitely do not think Harry Potter should be the domain of the 'CHILDREN ONLY', Leaky even has a section pointing the way to 'Potter Parties'. In July 2007 there will be the largest European convention for adult Potter fans ever. Trot along to the University of Westminster with your wand if you count yourself amongst the initiated. At Sectus 2007 there will be 'four days of presentations, panels, discussions and themed activities'. If that isn't true fandom then I don't know what true fandom is. And don't get me started on the many Harry Potter spoof sites (often with a pornographic angle) – though it has to be said that *MAD* magazine's 'Harry Potter and the Attention Deficit Disorder' sounds intriguing...

Fan blogs by genre

It is not just blogs about individual writers or characters that enjoy a particular status within the online community. Book blogs from authors and readers alike can be found for a wide variety of genres. There are blogs on comic novels such as Comic Book Galaxy and Yet Another Comics Blog, blogs that focus on non-fiction works of a religious or philosophical ilk such as First Things, blogs on cookery titles (see our fantastic new title by Clotilde Dusoulier, *Chocolate and Zucchini,* for example and spot the unashamed plug!). Book blogs exist for fans of romantic literature, fans of erotic literature (see Chapter 9) and fans of more 'literary' literature. But some genres lend themselves more easily to the format. And few will be surprised that sci-fi, gothic horror, fantasy and crime fiction count amongst the most well-represented genres of all.

'Do you believe in ghosts?' 'Of course!'

Gabrielle Faust's website (www.gabriellefaust.com) is a good example of just how serious horror fans and writers take their chosen genre and their preferred reading matter. This isn't just entertainment, this is a whole way of living, where style is all important. You can't just dip in and out of the darkness. Listing her favourite horror film directors as 'Riddley Scott – *Aliens*, David Lynch – *Eraserhead*, Neil Jordan – *Interview with the Vampire,* Danny Boyle – *28 Days Later,* David Fincher – *Seven*' and her favourite musicians as 'Leonard Cohen, Peter Murphy, Blue October, Concrete Blonde, Skid Row', Faust gives us an immediate idea of her artistic preferences and sure enough this gothic horror writer is a complete devotee to the form. In one post she describes the way that gothic horror writers such as herself live:

> The life of a writer is often a very lonely one. For days, sometimes even weeks, we squirrel ourselves away from the living world, hiding in our dark little caves with only our insanity to keep us company. We wait patiently for the Muses to spare us a moment of their time and toss us a beautiful kernel of insight, which we clutch to our breasts like Golem with the ring. Any distraction would shatter our focus thereafter as we toil away for hours on end, molding and sculpting this kernel until it is glistening in the sunlight we have not seen in days. Only then do we often see the flaws, however, and back to our caves we slink to beg the Muses for yet another chance for inspiration. Thousands upon thousands of words, reams and reams of fine white paper marked with red ink soon to be thrown into the recycle bin along with the other slaughtered ideas. Grisly and dismal it can be at times, driving one to the edge of insanity. Why, we have all seen *The Shining,* have we not?'

It is not all doom and gloom though.

> However, when the planets align and darlings that survive the massacre rise up in their full glory, when the synchronicity of concept and language hums its magnificent melody of perfection, there is no greater joy one can experience. It is this elation, this state of utter bliss, which we strive for as writers, that great 'Yes!' moment that justifies the isolation, the insanity and the sacrifice. The life of a writer is a brutal one and not for the weak of conviction. To dedicate one's self to this profession is to open one's soul to the criticisms of the masses; to endure the stones with the same graciousness as one accepts the praise. Let no one ever tell you it is 'easy' to be a writer. However, if one chooses this path they can be assured that it is also profoundly rewarding when times are good, satiating the restlessness of the spirit and quieting the demons that haunt us until the early hours before dawn…
>
> Nevertheless…it is still a very strange life…But vodka and cats do help, at times...

The highs and the lows of this particular writer are clearly more extreme than those of the average blogger!

Here's what Gabrielle has to say to those of us who aren't used to turning up at parties in full gothic regalia, and may be adverse to the wearing of masks on a Saturday night:

> Horror fans are a special breed of convention attendees. I have travelled to more than my fair share of conferences and conventions across the nation from sci-fi and fantasy to comic books and *anime*. And while I immensely enjoyed myself at each event, there is a special sensation of welcome that comes with attending a horror conference...with every convention, no matter the focus, there bubbles up to the surface a degree of ego that is often times over-cultivated in attendees who consider themselves 'experts' in whatever field it may be. To outsiders, those who do not consider themselves experts yet still possess an overwhelming curiosity to learn more, this wall between them and the world inside can come

off as arrogant and patronising causing many to steer clear of mass conventions for fear of being made to feel as if they are being looked down upon. I personally have always found this attitude amusing, if sometimes annoying. It is this attitude which you will rarely find at horror conventions...

For the outside observer, I can imagine that it can be an intimidating crowd to enter if they themselves are not black-clad, tattooed and pierced, but this should not deter the curious! Horror fans are some of the most kind, intelligent, insanely funny and honourable people I have ever met and I am proud to be able to say I am among their fold. This weekend further proved to me the power, not only of the horror world itself, but of the devotion and enthusiasm of the followers. It is what keeps me at my keyboard every day. It is what motivates me to dream bigger, travel further, and meet as many people at these conventions as I possibly can. The horror genre is alive and well and could not have a better support system beneath it. Horror fans, you are dark and beautiful in your insanity! Keep fighting the good fight! We owe it all to you!

Not all horror fans are quite so serious in their devotion to the cause. At The Horror Blog run by Steven Wintle (which isn't strictly a blog about books but they do feature heavily, hence the inclusion) when faced with the task of naming the one horror-related item that they couldn't bear to part with contributors come up with some fairly amusing results and many of them name their favourite books. Sean T Collins (or 'Attentiondeficitdisorderly Too Flat') writes that:

It's a tie between my big gigantic *Complete Books of Blood* hardcover, containing each and every one of Clive Barker's *BoB* short stories, which is out of print and awesome, and my advance readers' edition of *Barker's Coldheart Canyon*, which is autographed and contains an original Barker sketch AND a bunch of real-life character names that had to be altered to avoid litigation upon the book's actual publication. Sweet stuff both.

Jeff O'Brien find his pleasures at unlikely sources:

> Wow... I don't go for memorabilia but I have an old dog-eared copy of *Danse Macabre* by Stephen King that I read and reread time and again for enjoyment and inspiration.

and Curt of the Groovy Age of Horror writes:

> If you put it in terms of saving stuff if a fire broke out, I'd probably start with the top milk crate of paperbacks I haven't read yet.

Whereas Stacie (Final Girl) opts for her blog itself, which is calculated to make her seem big-hearted:

> Damn you and your 'one item'! I mean, which movie do I choose? Which book? Which autographed picture? This is too difficult.
>
> I'll just go with my beloved Freddy Krueger candle. I think it's probably irreplaceable, unlike mostly everything else.
>
> Or should I say my blog? Does that count? Maybe I'll say my blog. That's sweet and non-materialistic.

However, as Bill Cunningham (DisContent) says 'My brains' and Billy says 'CHAINSAWS!!!!', perhaps we should be careful about commenting on any of the answers here...scary stuff!

Horrific Schlock and more

For those of you who are not so good with tension and prefer a strain of comedy to lighten their experience of horror, 'Schlock Horror' might just provide the answer. The term is defined in the American Heritage Dictionary of English as 'Something, such as merchandise or literature, that is inferior or shoddy.' Possibly originating from Yiddish word '*shlak*' which means 'apoplexy, stroke, wretch, evil, nuisance', you can see how the term has been adapted to apply to any type of horror that is somewhat trashy, literature and films alike.

On the horror site 'Creatures of the Write' blogger Gabrielle Faust is named alongside Zombie Freak on its list of contributing writers, so it's not all schlock, but the main focus is *Danzmacabre*, an online fiction zine for horror, thrillers and splatterfest. The standard fare here is 'standalones' – horror stories that chill, thrill and make us shiver.

Bookgasm also casts its net-of-the-night wide enough to scoop up a healthy dose of schlock. Edited by Rod Lott and offering 'reading material to get excited about' Bookgasm aims to include coverage of all kinds of horror, schlock, comics, mystery writing, crime fiction and thrillers. With a picture of its founder on the home page – well, you can see his half his body reclining on a couch, his head is obscured by piles of paperbacks – the promise is that easily digestible reviews will guide you towards the very best in the genre: 'Because time isn't always kind: economic reviews in a world full of waste!' Or as the welcome page explains:

> Hey, have you read the new Nora Roberts?
>
> Are you a member of Oprah's Book Club?
>
> Do you enjoy stories about the struggles of the disenfranchised in our society?
>
> If you answered 'no' to all those questions, we'd like to welcome you to Bookgasm, the site dedicated to READING MATERIAL TO GET EXCITED ABOUT.
>
> That includes all kinds of genre fiction, from horror and sci-fi to mystery and suspense. It also includes graphic novels, trashy paperbacks, cheap magazines and other things that much of America pretends to be ashamed of, for no good reason.
>
> At Bookgasm we celebrate these escapist efforts, through daily

> news, reviews, interviews and other things that don't end in '-ews.' Think of it as a community; we encourage your posts via the comments section under each item.

For example we have the following post from contributor Matt Adder on July 11th 2007:

> If you're a zombie – or just into zombie porn – you'll dig DL Snell's novel from Permuted Press with a rather windy title: *Roses of Blood on Barbed Wire Veins*. Phew! Fortunately, anything that could be remotely connected to any of Anne Rice's boring bloodsucker books is absent. Instead, we get shock scene after shock scene, but there's enough of an underlying story to keep you moderately interested. *Roses* disturbs and titillates, but maybe not in the right order unless one is ready into this genre. Like Mexican wrestling, there's a niche for these kinds of stories and Snell revels in all its glory: Nazi zombies, sex swing amputees, zombie sex, vampires and – last but not least – an Uzi gun battle. Snell is an acquired taste and has skill, but if this were a movie, it would be a German snuff film. For those into shocking monster lit with heart – and brains and eyeballs – this is a quickly paced read.

Or try this for size: a quick run down of Tom Neely's *The Blot,* this time from Lott himself and posted that same month (in fact most reviews are written by Lott):

> Tom Neely's first graphic novel *The Blot* is one of those enigmatic, 'open to interpretation' exercises. Cleanly illustrated and virtually wordless, its sad-sack protagonist leaves home one day, only to encounter a massive but shapeless ink blot, which blacks out some scenery and spills from the eyes and mouths of people he meets. It haunts him at home, it chases him through the streets, it nearly swallows his girlfriend, it turns into a giant dog with tentacles, it makes him hurt himself. What does it all mean? I don't know,

> but I enjoyed being baffled. It's as if David Lynch moved into the wonderful world of Walt Disney. He succeeds at being puzzling...not to mention making ink blots terrifying and nudity look repulsive.

The Groovy Age of Horror

If you are particular about the type of horror you want to spend money on, and inclined towards retro goods, the Groovy Age of Horror is worth a look, as this blog focuses exclusively on vintage horror from the 60s and 70s, including paperbacks, comics, fumetti, Groschenromane, manga, magazines, etc. The aim is 'to cover the whole international scene across as many media as possible and to highlight what's defining and distinct about horror in this period.' Curt Purcell, who runs The Groovy Age of Horror (and also occasionally comments on US politics from a liberal perspective) blogs about his motivations in June 2006, explaining that he wants to create a fantasy world, a place to escape to that is moulded on his cult-horror ideal:

> In a sense, I'd like the story-worlds of all these novels I review to melt into one grand, sleazy, sexy, monster-haunted, cult-ridden, distinctly 1960s - 1970s world of groovy horror. And I'd like the images I post – whether paperback covers or fumetti or movie posters or screenshots – to serve as windows on that world. When you come here, I want you to feel like you're going to that place, and when you click away, I want you to feel like you've been somewhere dark, fun, and fascinating. That's the experience I'd love to evoke.

For an example of his discerning eye (this is not one of those 'optimistic blogs' that will try and praise everything), here's a review of MacLean's *Caravan To Vaccares* which definitely didn't get the thumbs up:

Alistair MacLean 'Master Storyteller' will no doubt be familiar to a lot of you, but this is my first reading of one of his novels. I don't believe this is one he's particularly noted for, and I was certainly underwhelmed.

I came to it hoping for a meticulously researched tale of murder, secrets, and intrigue within the world of Gypsies. I expected it to be full of authentic detail about their lives and codes and culture.

Well, that's not what I got. The Gypsies here are nothing but a cartoonish pack of swarthy villains. Neil Bowman is a James Bond knockoff who is trying to find out what nefarious no-good they're up to, and stop it. Then there's Le Grand Duc, a portly gourmand who's somehow mixed up with them, ostensibly as a folklorist. Oh, and there are two young ladies who are adorably feisty but ditzy and weak, who must frequently acquiesce to the smiling condescension of the men in the story. In the end, this turns out to be a fairly rote adventure of Cold War smuggling and espionage.

There's some decent action and suspense, but not enough to make this worth your time or money. Not recommended.

Alternatively, for some short sharp advice on Manga here's another recent post from contributor Kimberley Lindbergs:

***The Blood of Many Roses* by Akiko Jyo**

I decided to begin sharing some vampire manga with Groovy Age readers to follow up my previous post about Japanese horror manga. Vampire stories and films are popular in Japan and they often find inspiration in classic gothic tales from Europe and Britain.

This story was originally published in the popular Japanese shoujo ('girls') manga magazine *Ribon* in 1976. It's written and illustrated by a female artist named Akiko Jyo. I don't read or speak Japanese, but I've tried to translate the title as best as I could with the help of some trusty Japanese dictionaries. I believe the manga is called *The Blood of Many Roses*, but corrections are more than welcome!

Two important things to remember when trying to follow untranslated Japanese manga:

1. Male characters are often extremely effeminate looking and it can be hard to distinguish them from the female characters.
2. Unlike American and European comic books, Japanese manga stories are read from left to right.

If you still find you're stuck for horror blogs visit Where the Monsters Go, which is a comprehensive listing of everyone from Screamwriter to Horror Reader.

The weird and wonderful world of sci-fi

Although there are hundreds of sci-fi blogs, most spread their wings to cover film, TV, art and comics as well as books, so this section will pick out just one or two with more of a fiction-based bent than most. Once operating as The Alien Online, the UKSF Network is a website dedicated to science fiction book news with a UK bias, as they explain themselves:

> Our aim is to be the UK's go-to website for regularly-updated science fiction, fantasy and horror book news, comics and graphic novel news and more; with a definite focus on UK authors, writers, publishers and creators.

Along with pretty extensive review coverage of new sci-fi publications, a typical sample of the type of stories covered includes features on sci-fi author Richard Morgan's US tour for *Black Man* (or *Thirteen* in the US), the new *Penguin Sci-fi Omnibus* or information about the new online sci-fi writing project and fictional world 'Galaxiki' which invites everyone to create life forms, 'start editing stars, planets and moons, or get your own personal solar system.' Where else do you get to play god with such apparent ease?

Or if you are after something a little more bizarre, the post on the 'Year of Teledu' describes how a giant badger and friends have been running round sci-fi conventions of late trying to drum up interest in a one-off event taking place in Leicester this summer with a badgerish theme. Taking a somewhat extended break from event organisation since their Year of the Wombat convention in 1997, some ten years later the organisers are back in business, this time with something quite new: an open source convention. All are invited to arrange discussion groups, lectures and other events...but no, these don't have to involve badgers necessarily...

For an alternative 'portal to dark worlds' try www.shadowdark.org which has a sci-fi blog, horror search engine and e-book shop as well as Top 10 sci-fi books listing and reviews of sci-fi fantasy fiction. My favourite section here is, however, the interactive stories category where you can play an active part in the creation of stories like 'Dan, Ludwig and the Starship Terramaster' by mutant knife or 'Magnus the Roach' a story about a roach, a war and some talk about judgement day.

> SF Site is composed of many pieces. Twice a month since July 1997, we have posted a mixture of book reviews, opinion pieces, author interviews, fiction excerpts, author and publisher reading lists and a variety of other features. At the same time, we've maintained a comprehensive list of links to author and fan tribute sites, SF conventions, SF TV and movies, magazines and e-zines, writer resources, publishers and small press sites and many other SF resources.

But The Internet Review of Science Fiction is also pretty impressive. Run by L Blunt 'Bluejack' Jackson, this website and associated blog is undergoing a violent overhaul, so whilst readers are left with only a handful of short reviews of new fiction to tide them over, there is a valiant promise that all former glory will be surpassed in the not-too-distant future. Keep your mouse at the ready... See also Danny Yee's Book Reviews for a more personal touch. Writing from Australia about his declining taste in science fiction, Danny says:

> This isn't all the science fiction I've read, by any means. When I was at high school in the first half of the 1980s I read pretty much all the science fiction and fantasy in my local library – probably two or three thousand books. But I haven't read nearly as much since then, and I only started writing book reviews in 1992...

There is something quietly touching in this admission, I'm almost tempted to delve into his recommended list myself. Anyone for Julian May's *Jack the Bodiless*?

Romance Junkies

But now for a change in pace, something 'pleasant', something uplifting! (Well, in theory...) The romantic novel, the book blogger who continues to believe in happy endings, in love at first sight and the possibility of a soul mate – an unlikely entity, in this day and age? You'd be surprised. Cue Romance Junkies for starters.

A quick search on Google for this site yields the promise of links to 'book reviews, author biographies, a calendar of events, free postcards and Victorian calling cards'. Which all sounds quite fun, if romantic literature is your bag, but the home page features the most hideous smooth-talking animated host and introduction I've yet come across. (Everyone in the office shouts out 'Ugh! What's that?' when I open it.) Having said that, it does make you sit up and take notice when a small cartoon croons at you from the screen and the people at Romance Junkies must be doing something right – there were over a million hits recorded in April 2006, for example, which is a pretty astounding figure.

Romance Junkies, owned and operated from Arizona, US by

Cat Brown and Todd Pryor, has been listed in the *Writer's Digest* as amongst their '101 Best Websites for Writers' but readers of romantic novels are offered competitions, a book club, online discussions with their favourite authors and of course a run down on new titles, so don't assume this is just some sort of wannabe authors love-in. Romance Junkies is keen to support new writers, however, so the site states that all 80% of promotional opportunities are free. One click away and you can hear all about titles like *Tempt Me Tonight* by Toni Blake or the *Under the Covers* series for saucier readers.

Elsewhere (at www.likesbooks.com) you can find All About Romance (look out for the racy covers featured on the home page!) whose site is a self-declared 'labour of love' which aims to have something for all romance fans:

> ...from the smartest reviews (more than 6,000 of them!) you'll find anywhere to At the Back Fence, our must-read column for everyone who reads – and writes – romance, on to the liveliest message boards on the web, and so much more, All About Romance is your daily destination to find out who's who and what's what in romance fiction today.
>
> For those looking to join us 'after hours' visit AAR After Hours, our off-topic blog. It's where we go to kick back, relax and talk about everything, including what we're reading outside of books we review.

The idea here is to promote a highly relaxed atmosphere, reminiscent of neighbourly, over-the-fence chat:

> Our mission is to provide a back-fence atmosphere, a sense of community for lovers of romance novels, to provide honest, thoughtful and entertaining material in order to promote intelligent and diverse discussion about romance novels, and to help readers determine how best to spend their romance novel dollar...

There is also The Romance Reader which has categories on contemporary, historical and fantasy-orientated romantic novels, as well as the usual reviews (over 70,000 are included on the site) and interviews. The home page points you to its sister-site The Mystery Reader, in case you happen to be a fan of both. Romance: By The Blog is another popular site, along with Romantic Times, and for those of you who might be inclined to mock the traditions of the genre, with its formulaic plot lines, dashing heroes and swooning heroines, Daniela Licata at Romancing the Blog will set you straight in a recent post in deference of her favourite pastime, as well as advising on 'What's hip, what's now, what's tomorrow in the romance world.'

> Women who read romances, especially the old bodice rippers of yesteryear, are quite often stigmatised and viewed as unintelligent hicks, perhaps sexually deprived and/or sexually frustrated. We're quite often seen as living in some sort of dream world; our heads filled with so much unrealistic garbage, that we end up disappointed.
>
> You're living in la la land, dreamland, Disneyland...I've heard it all. And I'm tired of it. The erroneous assumptions and perceptions need to cease!
>
> Women who read romance novels are not unintelligent hicks; they're lawyers, doctors, librarians, housewives, mothers. And sexually deprived? Some lead very exciting and fulfilling sex lives; they don't need to get their kicks from literature. And what if some of us do? What's wrong with that? Why the bad rep? As for the high expectations? If there's one thing a good romance does, it's give us the right ones. Since when is wanting a man to love and cherish us, like the heroes of romance novels, a high expectation? What's wrong with wanting a man to be faithful to us, loyal to us, madly in love with us? Are we truly expected to settle for the ordinary?
>
> Romance novels may be perceived as hurting women, by leading

> them on to believe in a sort of fairy tale love, but I see them more as teaching women lessons in life. As silly as they seem, romance novels teach women, both young and old, the basic fundamentals of living.
>
> What do the women in romances refuse to do? SETTLE.
>
> What do women in romance novels fight for? RESPECT.
>
> What do they never compromise? THEMSELVES

And if you think this is an outdated mode of entertainment, log on to I Heart Harlequin, which celebrates all the titles from the 'Harlequin Presents' series. In a recent post its founder stands up for the female characters that her favourite writers create, arguing that the women in romantic fiction no longer conform to stereotypes, and certainly aren't the weak and timid creatures that the genre originally portrayed them as.

> A few weeks ago, we had a lively (!) discussion about the Alpha male hero in Harlequin Presents romances. So let's now consider the Presents heroine.
>
> When I started reading Presents as a teenager, the heroines of the series were emerging from an age when they had been 'nice gels' as we say in England: prim, virginal, often sheltered and without a profession, though if they did work, it was in a role, such as nanny, governess or companion. It's easy to smile when we think about these heroines of yesteryear, and yet they were important symbols to readers then, personifying certain emotions and fantasies – for instance, the unworldly ugly duckling who emerged a swan, or the young woman who experienced emotional and (in a euphemistic way) sexual awakening.
>
> Those of us who are regular Presents readers these days know that our heroines have evolved a long, long way since, though at their cores they still retain echoes of their forebears. For example, Lynne Graham's heroines continue to be Cinderellas at heart, but

in a wholly contemporary way: they battle with their weight, know about surviving in a lowly job on a minimum wage and the potential heartbreak that being pregnant and alone can bring; Miranda Lee's heroines operate at the other end of the spectrum – they're city girls negotiating the urban jungles of cosmopolitan Sydney, often with little sexual experience and not looking for Mr Right, but at heart they're as soft and vulnerable as the next woman and hoping one day to settle down to marriage and children.

What is important to readers today is that Presents heroines reflect their aspirations, emotions, victories and struggles; the reader wants to see pieces of herself. So, Sandra Marton's female protagonists are always popular because they don't take their heroes' arrogances lying down; they start out wanting equality and a big part of their conflict – as they tame their men – is to get it!

Bloggers who turn to crime

Sarah Weinman, whom we mentioned earlier for being one half of Galley Cat, is also the blogger behind Confessions of an Idiosyncratic Mind. Though she announces that, 'My interests run the gamut from crime fiction to klezmer, from publishing to music, forensic science to gossip,' and includes lots of links and info on the publishing scene in the US, her blog is definitely best known for its in depth coverage of crime fiction and mystery writing. Formed in 2003, on a whim, Weinman says she just happened to be in the right place at the right time when she started her blog – and it really took off. Having no idea that it would be so successful, she is now widely regarded as the best mystery critic on the web and her blog is read closely by mystery writers, editors and publishers alike. She appears on panels at mystery conventions and now writes reviews for major print publications. She has also written short stories for independent publisher Akashic Books, New York. Here's a few samples reviews taken from her 'picks of the week':

Amanda Eyre Ward: *Forgive Me: A Novel*

The ending doesn't quite deliver as I expected but the first 200-odd page are about as brilliant as I've read in a while. I could literally feel myself getting lost in Ward's understated yet driven prose that seems to dive so deep into the hearts and minds of her characters and their many, many flaws. It's about forgiveness, about self-acceptance (and the lack thereof) and most important, about how there are no absolutes in life – even about the most horrific subjects.

Anthony Flacco: *The Last Nightingale: A Novel of Suspense*

Historical suspense set in the immediate aftermath of the 1906 Earthquake? Of course I'm going to read it. What results is a fast-moving tale of serial killing when almost no one is looking, caught as they are in the midst of a seeming apocalyptic nightmare. Where Flacco especially shines in his depiction of the two children, newly orphaned Shane Nightingale and the plucky girl who calls herself Vignette in order to give herself a more mysterious air. I haven't been hearing much about this book at all and that's a shame - it's clearly deserving of a very wide audience.

Jason Pinter: *The Mark*

There are many reasons to read this book: the trials and tribulations of neophyte journalist Henry Parker; the developing chemistry between Parker and his forged-in-fire friend, Amanda Davies; the visceral writing style and sly knocks on a world where celebrity of any kind gives you credibility. But most of all, read it because if you do, you won't be able to stop. At least, I couldn't.

Olen Steinhauer: *Victory Square*

Steinhauer closes his five-book series of espionage-tinged novels set in Eastern Europe with a flourish, circling back to Emil Brod (the earnest protagonist of the Edgar-nominated *The*

> *Bridge of Sighs)* now sixty-four and very much feeling his age, the impending collapse of Cold War tactics and incoming change both professionally and personally. Of course there are loose strands dangling but here, as before, Steinhauer demonstrates why he's one of the smartest, most thoughtful crime novelists to emerge in recent years.

But Weinman doesn't just review the latest releases, she also keeps crime and mystery fans up to date on other happenings in their field, with gossip on industry awards like as the Daggers, or this post on the film of the thriller *Gone, Baby, Gone*, for example:

> Boston writer Dennis Lehane is giving big ups to Ben Affleck's big-screen adaptation of his 1998 kidnap thriller *Gone, Baby, Gone* saying the Cambridge homey has made a flick that 'reeks of Boston.'
>
> 'I saw the movie and it's terrific,' said Lehane who got a sneak peek at the made-in-Boston drama in New York City a few weeks back. 'I wasn't gonna say anything if I didn't like it but it's really terrific.'
>
> Lehane said Affleck, who directed the movie and adapted the screenplay, was 'over the moon' when he gave him his film review. 'The plan was, if I hated it, I'd vanish,' he said. 'I actually set up my schedule to go into a black hole in September and October. But I gotta tell you, I'm very, very happy.'

And if that isn't enough of a crime writing fix for you, The Idiosyncratic Mind also includes links to around thirty more bloggers on crime fiction, including booksnbytes, Crime Time, Euro Crime and Crime Spot – which in turn links you to another fifty or thereabouts. There is clearly something about the psyche of the crime fiction fan that lends itself to blogging. See Muderati, The Little Blog of Murder, The Mystery Chicks, Mystery*File

Blog, LA Noir, Crime Fiction Dossier, Girl Detective, Crimedog One and The Thrilling Detective Blog. I also like the sound of The Good Girls Kill for Money Club. Well, its not such a bad idea...

For a European perspective it is also worth checking out Finnish writer Juri Nummelin's Pulpetti. At the tender age of thirty-five he has already written a number of books on the history of cinema, rare first names, western writers and food, but pulp fiction is his real passion. That he really knows his stuff is self-evident, take a look at this post about finding a rare magazine at a flea market, as you will almost see him salivating, the enthusiasm is so infectious:

> Boy oh boy, was I lucky today! I was at the flea market at the Turku open marketplace where people sell their own stuff during Summer and spotted a couple of old Viikonloppu/Weekend fiction magazines from the late 50s. Normally they hold no interest for me, as there usually are no authors' names and the stuff that was published in the mag was almost exclusively women's romance. But then I thought, what the heck, you never know, there might be something. I asked what they cost and an old lady said 'fifty cents a piece' (which is, if I remember my currencies correctly, forty American cents).
>
> The first one I flipped through yielded nothing, but then – then, in the issue 28/1958, I noticed a familiar name in a story: Ki-Gor. The story was called 'The Gods of Atlantis/Atlantiksen jumalat.'
>
> Then I noticed the writer's name: John Peter Drummond. Then I realised that I'd found something I didn't earlier know to have been published in Finnish: a translation of a Ki-Gor story from the *Jungle Stories* pulp magazine. I'd written about the Ki-Gor stories in Pulp, my fanzine that deals with all things pulp, as part of my longer article of Tarzan copycats. But I sure didn't know that the Finnish audience had been in access to read the

genuine article themselves!

Now, for those who don't know: Ki-Gor appeared in a pulp magazine called *Jungle Stories* from 1939 to 1954. It was one of the most popular Tarzan copycats that was seen also in comic books, only with his name changed into Kaanga. (Don't really know why this was.) The first of the stories was written by John M. Reynolds, but the rest of the adventures were written by John Peter Drummond that was a house pseudonym. Ki-Gor is Robert Kilgour who's orphaned when his parents die – they are missionaries working in Africa. Ki-Gor is rescued by a bunch of animals and he develops into an athlete. He finds a young lady called Helene Vaughn whose plane is wrecked and they fall in love. Ki-Gor's best friends are Timbu George, who's a black African, and N'Geeso, a pygmy chief. Ki-Gor has a pet ape and an elephant on which he rides. So, basically he's Tarzan with another name.

Some of the Ki-Gor stories have been recently reprinted. Here's also some stuff on Ki-Gor, and it reveals that the Finnish translation was originally called 'The Beast Gods of Atlantis' and it was originally published in the Winter 1949 issue of *Jungle Stories* (and reprinted in High Adventure,71, 2003).

I have to admit that I am amongst 'those of you who don't know' that Ki-Gor was basically Tarzan with another name, but with offers of free magazines – Nummelin very sweetly says he has got some copies of the *Jungle Stories* if anyone is interested – I might just turn a blind eye to the apparent plagiarism. Or perhaps I am being very naïve here: these issues are really collectors' items and in fact Nummelin is looking to make some fast cash.

Regardless, his blog makes for some interesting reading, if for no other reason than as an example of the in-depth knowledge and passion that fan bloggers have for their chosen field/idols. In this excerpt from the blog, for example, Nummelin mentions casually that he is typing up and translating from the Finnish pulp horror stories from the late 30s and 40s, apparently, just for the sheer hell of it.

> **An excerpt of Harry Etelä's short story**
> I've been editing and typing a collection of Harry Etelä's pulp horror stories from the late 30s and late 40s, as I've mentioned some times before. I've got only one to go (I've been typing these for the last two or three months, a page or two before actual work) and it's one of the fiercest stories ever published in Finnish language. It's a story about a village blacksmith who kidnaps young boys and grills them over fire and eats them! This was in 1939, in Finland, where decorum, a sense of decency, was pretty much ruling. Bad taste was something so despicable you can't even begin to describe it. (And bear in mind that Etelä also wrote some of the most revered and loved schlager tunes in Finland, such as Katri Helena's 'Puhelinlangat laulaa' (which was first recorded by his big brother, Pentti Viherluoto).
>
> Here's an excerpt of the story 'Kauhujen salakammio/The Secret Chamber of Horrors' that I've been thinking about would be the titular story of the collection. I'll translate the relevant bits after the Finnish part:
>
> > Ennen kuin poika käsittikään oli häneen tartuttu kourin, joitten hirmuinen voima oli rusentaa murskaksi hänen jäsenensä, ja hän tunsi sinkoutuvansa kammion toiseen päähän. Pudottuaan lattialle hän jäi makaamaan siihen liikkumattomana ja katseli salavihkaa käsivartensa yli, kuinka seppä hiipi lähemmäksi. Kun hän oli tullut yli keskilattian, poika nousi nopeasti ja juoksi kaartaen ovelle, jonka raskasta salpaa hän yritti kohottaa... [the Finnish continues here]
>
> > 'You gotta have a good fire, young hero,' he [the blacksmith] said. 'It is so nice to see, when you crumble in and get so

> sweet and brown. I'll eat the best parts of you today, the rest I will take down to the cellar. You know that I like the palms most?'
>
> The boy heard the chains and iron bars rattle. Now he understood the meaning of the rings... he would be hung over the fire...

For the love of reading

A quick tour through the vast array of fan blogs and genre blogs available on the internet swiftly hammers home the point that book blogging is not just about self-promotion or self-aggrandisement. With regards to the motivation behind book blogging there is a good quote from one blogger, volunteer contributor Emily Dixon posted at The Reader. Whilst the mission at The Reader is 'bringing books to life', 'to promote the good in literature, with the belief that books can be serious and fun, life-enhancing and creative for everyone,' Dixon's comments on the power of the novel in terms of creating an alternative reality certainly fit the bill:

> For me, the escapism part of reading belongs to the act itself; the images that this act creates are not simply an alternative reality in which to get lost, but importantly form a world that, though separate, belongs to our own, and reflects back onto it. This is a world that can be powerful enough to make us think about ourselves as individuals, affecting our emotions, but in doing so, also making us question the feelings themselves, where they have come from, and to whom they (should) belong.

But she also has a few words to say on why she likes blogging about books, that sum up much of what we've found concerning why people blog. In Dixon's case, she simply enjoys sharing what she's read as much as reading itself...

> For me, one of the greatest pleasures of reading comes from being able to share my thoughts and feelings about a novel with those around me. Though it doesn't generally stop me talking if my audience isn't interested (I'm always hopeful of converting a non-reader to the magical world of books – at least, that's my excuse!), I'm especially delighted when my chosen subject has either read the book and wants to discuss it, or is inspired to go on to read and (hopefully) enjoy it. Of course, this enthusiasm is also generated when the roles are reversed and people recommend novels to me...

I remarked earlier on the fact that 'it's a two-way thing', this book blogging business. But I'm being too short-sighted here. A vast network lies behind the many individual post on individuals titles that bloggers contribute to their own and others' sites. Within a forum on 'Why Do We Blog?' Anne Mathewson of US media design agency Fishbucket writes:

> Herman Meville put it best when he said, 'We cannot live for ourselves alone. Our lives are connected by a thousand invisible threads and along these synthetic fibers, our actions run as causes and return to us as results' A perfect description of blogging, don't you think?
>
> I started blogging some years ago to pass the time and share experiences. A small part of me, however, was selfishly hoping for admiration and affirmation; a shallow attitude I've long abandoned. Eventually, I discovered the joy found via 'invisible threads' and 'sympathetic fibres' – those human connections made along the way...'

And on that quasi-spiritual note about the joy of sharing, I'll be off... (she does have a point though...)

Rebecca Gillieron

Blogs on erotic literature: a taste for the extreme

Everyone knows that one of the first uses for the internet was the distribution of pornography, mainly erotic photographs, which I assume people were attracted to since they could look at them in the privacy of their own homes. For a while, before anti-spam, virus and pop-up software became available, our PC at home would be plagued by the sudden arrival of rude photographs which frankly did nothing for me and even less, I imagine, for my two young daughters. These have thankfully disappeared and as we are now Mac users we seem to get fewer intrusions onto our desktop.

However, books which arise from blogs about people's intimate moments have been a roaring success. I like to see young women reading *Belle de Jour* on the bus as if it is a work of great intellectual calibre.

Ms Belle de Jour's writing style is a perfect example of the blog, which with the addition of a little extra imagination on the part of the reader, becomes suggestive and sexy. It is however, still a blog, and is not the same as 'literary pornography'. Actually, even to be making up, as I write, a genre called 'literary pornography' shows how far we have come in liberalism. A few years ago, *literary* would have been a term applied to all things good, in the world of letters, and *pornography* would have been a form of writing to be banned, taken off the shelves, and hidden away. So why isn't *Belle de Jour* 'literary pornography' of the highest type? Consider the following entry:

> Met a client near Waterloo. I decided on top-to-toe white, mainly because I'd just bought a new lace basque, also because all my other stockings had ladders. He'd booked two hours which either means they want something odd or they want conversation.
>
> This was the latter. We drank our way through two bottles of chilled chardonnay, discussed the Sultan of Brunei's gambling habits and listened to the latest releases from Coldplay and Dido.

He had loads of fluffy towels and a giant bath for afterward, and we ate crisps and drank wine a full hour past when I was supposed to go. It's not often I feel the cab's turned up too soon. It's even rarer I give someone my direct number.

Nabbed a nice cabbie for the way home. He was from Croydon, and we chattered about Orlando Bloom, new year's fireworks and Christmas parties. I told him I worked at a well-known accountancy firm. I don't think he was fooled for a second.

And this:

Snow yesterday afternoon – near UCL, students dashed out of the Union and Archaeology to gather up handfuls of snow and throw them at each other. Clusters of girls walked by in twos and threes, huddling under umbrellas. Though it had gone dark, the light was calm, diffuse: a warm glow of streetlights reflecting off the puffy duvet-sized flakes coming down.

I went to meet one of the other As (A2), who hasn't had a date any time this geological era. He recently hooked up with someone at a conference, though, a girl from Manchester. It seems a long way to go for sex. He assures me it isn't just about the sex. A2 is a great chap, but an extremely poor liar.

We installed ourselves in a gastropub-cum-bar to watch the buses outside pile up in the icy street. It was one of these places with a high ratio of leather seating to bar space where they turn up the music automatically at 7pm, regardless of how many customers are inside. We were practically shouting over the background noise to hear each other.

'So what do you think of latex?' A2 bellowed.

'Latex?' I asked, unsure if I misheard. 'A good idea, generally.' Unhappily, I am discovering a recent sensitivity to the stuff, having come away from a blowjob at work with swollen, tingling lips. Hardly a scientific experiment, though. It could just as easily have been the spermicide on the Durex.

'No, I mean like – ' he mimed putting on a rubber glove. 'Latex. The feel of it, you know, for –'

'You're talking about rubber sex already?'

'She's a hell of a girl,' he mused. 'So, have you ever done it?'

The squeaky squeaky? 'Not full coverage, no. You mean with the catheter and head mask and everything? No.' Ugh. 'Up your urethra' is probably the least arousing phrase I can imagine, ever.

'I so want to go there.'

'Careful, you'll scare her off.'

'It was her idea. So – tips?'

'Lots of baby powder, I should think. I don't even want to think about what this would smell like.'

'Mmm, I do.'

Where do people come up with this stuff? And wouldn't it get rather sweaty in there? 'Freak. You said this was – and I quote – not just a sex thing.'

'Takes one to know one.'

'Who, me?' I put a hand to my chest in mock surprise. 'I would absolutely never. I'm as pure as the you-know-what,' I said, nodding toward the snow outside.

'Sure you wouldn't. You having another?' A2 yelled over a godawful cover song by Blue.

'Something hot, if they have it. With plenty of alcohol. Only way to banish this music. And the mental image of you humping a blow-up doll.'

When placed alongside our very own George Bataille they are different kinds of writing - the blog is all so much more companionable and easy. You do not have to make a great deal of effort to understand it, which I why it has been bought by many thousands of young women who have had a very enjoyable read. I don't know – the idea of having sex with a rubber doll just sounds a little desperate to me. This all sounds amusing and jolly, rather than ground-breakingly erotic. However, here are extracts from two of our erotic novels, which I think are a little more on the exciting side. The writing is undoubtedly challenging, though:

Georges Bataille, *The Story of the Eye***, 1928**
Simone gradually emerged from her stupor and sought protection with Sir Edmund, who stood motionless, his back to the wall; we could hear the fly flitting over the corpse.

'Sir Edmund,' she said, rubbing her neck gently on his shoulder, 'I want you to do something.'

I shall do anything you like,' he replied.

She made me come over to the corpse: she knelt down and completely opened the eye that the fly had perched on.

'Do you see the eye?" she asked me.

'Well?'

'It's an egg,' she concluded in all simplicity.

'All right,' I urged her, extremely disturbed, 'what are you getting at?'

'I want to play with this eye.'

'Listen, Sir Edmund," she finally let it out, "you must give me this at once, tear it out at once, I want it!'

Sir Edmund was always poker-faced except when he turned purple. Nor did he bat an eyelash now; but the blood did shoot to his face. He removed a pair of fine scissors from his wallet, knelt down, then nimbly inserted the fingers of his left hand into the obstinate ligaments. Next, he presented the small whitish eyeball in a hand reddened with blood.

Simone gazed at the absurdity and finally took it in her hand, completely distraught; yet she had no qualms, and instantly amused herself by fondling the depth of her thighs and inserting this apparently fluid object. The caress of the eye over the skin is so utterly, so extraordinarily gentle, and the sensation is so bizarre that it has something of a rooster's horrible crowing.

Simone meanwhile amused herself by slipping the eye into the profound crevice of her arse, and after lying down on her back and raising her legs and bottom, she tried to keep the eye there simply by squeezing her buttocks together. But all at once, it spat out like a stone squeezed from a cherry, and dropped on the thin belly of the corpse, an inch or so from the cock....

But finally, Simone left me, grabbed the beautiful eyeball from the hands of the tall Englishman, and with a staid and regular pressure from her hands, she slid it into her slobbery flesh, in the midst of the fur. And then she promptly drew me over, clutching my neck between her arms and smashing her hips on mine so forcefully that I came without touching her and my come shot all over her fur.

Now I stood up and, while Simone lay on her side, I drew her thighs apart, and found myself facing something I imagine I had been waiting for in the same way that a guillotine waits for a neck to slice. I even felt as if my eyes were bulging from my head, erectile with horror; in Simone's hairy vagina, I saw the van blue eye of Marcelle, gazing at me through tears of urine. Streaks of come in the steaming hair helped give that dreamy vision a disastrous sadness. I held the thighs open while Simone was convulsed by the urinary spasm, and the burning urine streamed out from under the eye down to the thighs below....

Now this to my mind is scary, shocking, definitely bordering on the insane and one would have to classify it as erotic, if not exactly titillating, seeing as it is closer to a horror story rather than a romantic episode.

Hong Ying, in *K: The Art of Love,* set standards high for gentle, feminine erotica in the relationship between Lin and Julian Bell. Julian Bell is a teacher of English in China, before the First World War, and he has an affair with the wife of a professor. In Peking, after several false starts, they eventually find a hotel room where they can be alone together:

He had waited so long to see Lin's naked body – now, at last, he gazed at it. She was perfectly proportioned, and her skin shone with a warm., golden glow, almost as if it were not of flesh and blood. He was amazed to see that she had no trace of hair in her armpits, not did she have any pubic hair at all. When he eased her legs apart the lips of her vulva opened up to his eyes like two long petals, converging into the whorl of her clitoris.

Julian had never seen a woman's pudenda so nakedly exposed. It looked to him more like a work of art than a real human body. He was sweating profusely, as excited as a boy during his first sexual experience.

He shifted his gaze to her hair on the pillow: it framed her face and shoulders like black silk. His hand began to wander over her, touching lightly and carefully. He was fascinated by her breasts, prominent and full, with a texture like ivory. They seemed to have a sculptural quality finer that any he had ever seen on his mother's life models. And her skin, from her head to her feet, was smooth as satin. He held her close to him. Lin kept her hands pressed tightly over her face, preventing him from kissing her mouth, but he grasped her right breast in one hand and took her left nipple in his mouth. He let his free hand explore the rest of her body, from her waist to her stomach, hips and legs. As his hand moved to touch her prominent clitoris, she moaned and he found that she was warm and wet. In an ecstasy of delight he pulled her hand away from her face and kissed her full on the mouth.'

It's rare to find a woman writing erotic prose which actually focuses on the woman's pleasure. I do not really understand why most pornography is about the male experience, I am very doubtful about books where a male protagonist works his way through several teenage girls, who are all desperate to be pleasured by him. Or the same teenage girl has a multitude of relationships with men who are ships passing in the night emerging ready for a new day with barely an emotional scar. In my experience, women are not like this. Women have relationships with people, rather than encounters and do not often fancy men in their fifties when they are still in their teens. But perhaps I am just old fashioned.

When *The Sexual Life of Catherine Millet* was being offered to English publishers, it came into this office and I sat down one rainy day to read it in French. I can read most French but I did have to resort to the dictionary for a few words – *mamelon* (nipple), gland (tumour – I guess erection, no, that must be *l'engourdissement,* no that actually means numbness, which is what I think happens when you have been lying down too long). However, for Mme Millet, '*engourdisement gagné* – wins (her vagina). Others were beyond my linguistic experience. But you can see what fun it was trying to fathom it out, and all in the interest of work and making an editorial decision. All I can remember about that day was tears of laughter coursing down my face as I imagined every encounter Mme Millet had at various gatherings, where it seemed that every orifice was up for invasion by another male human being. At least this book was published before the book blog got going, or else I can imagine a lot of parents having to block her urls.

Where *Belle de Jour* does win, however, is in its cover design, and in the whole package of accessible writing for women, in an erotic vein. Although there have been several editions, most sport swirly pink type, and a glittering shoe, thus marking them undoubtedly as books for young women. I feel quite good about the fact that today's young women will read erotic books in public. In contrast, the cover of *The Sexual Life of Catherine Millet* is black with plain type, which must be the closest to publishing a brown paper bag. Our own edition of *K: The Art of Love* has a subtle pink cover with the naked backside of a girl, covered in Chinese blossom. Our cover was mimicked the world over when we sold foreign rights, which I see as a compliment. However, it is quite gentle and does not really convey the message that this book is a sexual riot. This is probably just as well, since there is a story as well as the erotic content in this novel.

If I was to analyse further the different mental athletics which go on internally when you are writing for the internet, or writing a book, I could generalise and say that writing for a book is a far more deliberated activity. There is time to review your draft, take a step back, and rewrite for clarity. With the internet, you write a blog entry, get a chance to preview, and then with basic mistakes corrected, you just have to press a button, called 'Publish'. Then it's done, out for all to read. It's a quick process, which makes it easy to project your personality. But I would say that real art takes longer to achieve, and the best erotic literature is art.

Catheryn Kilgarriff

The Literary Establishment and its Blogs

The place to find independent writing is in the lists of the independent presses, who rely on reviews in the main quality broadsheets. We would expect to find independent publishers with blogs on their websites and writers with their own websites. We would also expect to find journalists flourishing online. Often, for instance, the *Guardian* online starts important news stories which then are picked up in the print media. However, we know that the official line is that writing which appears online is somehow inferior to that which appears in print. So it is with some joy that we can include the first blogs of a pair of literary establishment seniors, who have dared to join the same blogosphere which the independent sector has adopted with alacrity.

The subjects they cover are not just the concerns of large company economics or the obituaries of esteemed literary figures like Kurt Vonnegut (although I find both these subjects interesting for a while). They can be just as varied as the websites of the truly independent minds.

Richard Charkin keeps a blog on the Macmillan books website (charkinblog.macmillan.com). He is the Managing Director of the extremely successful house Pan Macmillan. His blog entries are often corporate, and he seems to have an enviable life travelling from Africa, Mexico and other outposts of the Macmillan empire.

You would assume from reading most of the blogs that

Macmillan always got things right – whether it is selling text books on English as a foreign language or launching the Macmillan New Writing Awards in which novelists get tuppence for the joy of having their novels published. Apparently 8000 would-be novelists entered the competition. This is somewhat mind boggling, and I will keep this figure in mind in case I am ever tempted to run a similar competition. I think it would take several lifetimes to read 8000 novels. I wouldn't be able to help thinking that the one I skipped would be the one that broke all records when it turned up on another publisher's list. Here is Richard Charkin deliberating about how wrong we can be about the future, by comparing forecasts from the 1950s to now.

April 15th 2007

Print is dead?

One of my favourite columnists is Matthew Parris. His latest piece is entitled 'So much for world progress. We have failed. We're stuck.' It promotes the contrarian view that there has actually been little progress in the last fifty years in the West (accepting that developing countries have seen significant change). He also referenced this link to the February 1950 issue of *Modern Mechanics* magazine predicting how the world will be in 2000. The predictions are, by and large, wrong. Here is one paragraph which is fairly typical.

> When Jane Dobson cleans house she simply turns the hose on everything. Why not? Furniture (upholstery included), rugs, draperies, unscratchable floors – all are made of synthetic fabric or waterproof plastic. After the water has run down a drain in the middle of the floor (later concealed by a rug of synthetic fiber) Jane turns on a blast of hot air and dries everything. A detergent in the water dissolves any resistant dirt. Tablecloths and napkins are made of woven paper yarn so

> fine that the untutored eye mistakes it for linen. Jane Dobson throws soiled "linen" into the incinerator. Bed sheets are of more substantial stuff, but Jane Dobson has only to hang them up and wash them down with a hose when she puts the bedroom in order.'

> This got me thinking about our ability to predict and how hopeless we probably are. We all remember predictions for the paperless office. Ha. Remember when libraries were going to get rid off all books and replace them with microfilm? Ha.
>
> However, sneakily things do change (usually in an unpredicted fashion) and book publishing is changing. Last year we commissioned Jeff Gomez who is head of internet marketing at Holtzbrinck Publishers USA to write a book about these changes. It's called *'Print is Dead'* and will be published in print form this Autumn (or Fall). As part of writing the book Jeff has set up the brilliant Print is Dead blog.
>
> > More than any other time in history, mankind faces a crossroads. One path leads to despair and utter hopelessness. The other, to total extinction. Let us pray we have the wisdom to choose correctly.

The literary editor who was first off the mark to join the blogosphere was Peter Stothard of the *Times Literary Supplement*. His blog is lively and erudite, and last year I was happy to find the contents of it adding to real life, as he referred to a lecture on Sappho that Germaine Greer gave, which I had attended. It was the address to the audience for the annual translation prizes given at the Sebald Lecture and in it Germaine Greer attacked the translation of a new Sappho poem which had recently been published in the *Times Literary Supplement*. The following comment posts are delightful, in that one relishes the image of the host's hand being bitten and the second learned gentleman eagerly posting about his forthcoming academic lecture on the same subject, thus jumping on the Sappho bandwagon.

October 4th 2005

Not Sapphic for Germaine

When Germaine Greer bites her host's hand, she does it so elegantly he hardly knows that his fingers have fallen off.

There I am last night, cheerfully giving the TLS prizes for literary translation at the Bloomsbury Theatre in London – and recalling proudly what has been our best 'translator' moment of the past few months, even years, the new poem by Sappho, reported by Martin West of All Souls, Oxford, in our TLS edition of June 24th.

Then up comes Professor Greer on to the stage to give the Sebald Lecture on a theme of literary translation. And she chooses Sappho.

How thoughtful, I think. I am almost waiting to hear 'and first some praise for our sponsor', or something like that.

But Professor Greer soon makes clear her dim view of male professors in ancient universities who think they know who Sappho was, what she might have written and why she might have written it.

As for the TLS poem, attributed to the 'middle aged Sappho', it is an implausible mixture of different fragments, assembled according to no logic that she can see, and wholly unworthy in any case. TLS readers have already been able to read two contemporary poet translators who seemed to disagree.

The audience is rapt at her bravura. The TLS Editor is rapt at her bravura, though quietly wondering why there is so much blood on his hosting hand.

No more details now. An article based on Professor Greer's speech will appear, I hope, in a future edition of the TLS and we can take on the argument from there.

Comments

I confess this has little to do with Sappho, but Greer biting her host's hand reminded me of an incident I read of in Lindy Woodhead's double biography of Elizabeth Arden and Helena Rubenstein 'War Paint' (published by Virago).

Apparently, Arden was a miserable, ill-tempered lady. Hard to work for, and not easy to get along with. Her staff feared her greatly.

However, she was remarkably transformed when spending time around her beloved horses. Loving, affectionate, happy. So much so that when one of her horses actually bit off half of one of her fingers during a feeding, she calmly took the finger, had it sewn back on and acted as if nothing had happened. Her horsekeepers were mortified, thinking they would either be fired or the horse would be put down.

It was as if nothing had happened.

But it is a brave horse that manages to bite the hand of its feeder.

Posted by Gemma Mahadeo

28th November 2005

Dear Peter,

This ceremony sounds like a wonderful event! However, I can offer a new interpretation of the poem, which 'is' in my view by Sappho, and I will hope eventually to be able to persuade Ms Greer and other sceptics as to its excellence.

As one of your poet-translators brings out, the poem has a careful tripartite structure and placement of imagery. But above all, it uses the myth of Tithonus to evoke the poetic immortality of the speaker even as her body ages. This evocation works because, in the myth that Sappho would already have known, the aged Tithonus, who cannot in his human form have immortality, turns into a cicada which sings beautifully for ever.

Thus the poem is much more subtle than first appears. It is absolutely in Sappho's voice; other fragments of hers also lay claim to her poetic immortality – which this discovery now gives back to her. I shall be giving a public lecture on this topic at a Symposium in honour of David Armstrong at the University of Texas in Austin on October 29th.

Yours sincerely,
Richard Janko
(Professor of Classical Studies, University of Michigan)

Still on the subject of creative women, Peter Stothard recently discussed the efforts of Jerry Hall in the poetry department, since she joined Hugo Williams's poetry class. I can recall one year in which she was suddenly one of the judges on the then Whitbread prize, so I was not entirely fazed by her incarnation as a 20th century poet. However, her poetry, as recorded in the press, which may or many not be true, is not great. In my mind her small fragment of poetry is really negligible. But in the mind of Stothard, it quickly became linked with the 16th century poet, Martial, who also had his axe to grind about marital pleasures. Jerry's poem is, we all suppose, about her erstwhile husband who:

fucks their women
and fights their battles against mediocrity
but when he comes home to me
all that's left is vd.

April 29th 2007

Something between Martial and Jerry Hall's mother?

Maid in the living room, cook in the kitchen, whore in the bedroom.

A blogger cannot mention Jerry Hall, it seems, without getting readers' reminders of what is her most famous quote, some words of womanly advice on how to hold on to her man.

Much as Ms Hall's latest poem has been appreciated by her fans, it seems unlikely that any product of Hugo Williams' composition classes will surpass her earlier verbal efforts.

To quote those in full:

'My mother said it was simple to keep a man, you must be a maid in the living room, a cook in the kitchen and a whore in the bedroom. I said I'd hire the other two and take care of the bedroom bit.'

Ah well.

But we're sticking to the literary stuff in this blog.

It's worth noting, since poetry classes are famously tough on plagiarism, that Ms Hall claimed no originality for the first part of her quote. Her mother is given the glory for that. The idea of the room-time-and-role-swap line came originally, I suppose, from Martial, that favourite author here – in a male formulation.

There are probably earlier cases. There are always earlier cases.

I don't have a text with me now but the speaker in Martial's poem (Bk 11 Ep 105) complains that his wife was failing to provide him with unorthodox sexual opportunities – sodomy in this case – which even the severest matrons of the past had freely granted.

He was happy, he wrote, with a respectable Roman Lucretia in the living room.

But he wanted a whorish Greek Lais in the bedroom.

The kitchen did not in those days come into the equation.

'If gravity by day doth thee delight, Lucretia be; I'll have thee Lais by night.'

In words which I can find this evening – from Robert Fletcher's translation of Martial, published in 1656.

I wonder what happened to the thought between 17th century England and 20th century Texas.

There are many individual journalists who have blogs, and some of them are worth finding (Sam Leith and India Knight are two). However, I think Stothard and Charkin are the only two industry figure heads who have dared air their views in public rather than at the lunch table. I wonder how badly other luminaries want to start a blog, but do not dare.

Catheryn Kilgarriff

The Internet and its Uses: Dialogues about Freedom of Expression and Personal Interest

Is the internet free?

'We never learnt how to route money.' David Clark MIT

The internet is an inherently free facility but that does not stop the huge players trying to make money out of it. The internet economy has different rules and it changes the parameters of normal trade. It's provides an environment within which you are allowed to browse for as long as you like without the watchful eye of a sales person. It is easy to block pop ups, so intrusive advertising, apart from being rather hopeless at selling anything, can be stopped. We can surf websites for free until we come across articles which we are asked to pay for. We can choose not to progress the transaction, and move on until we find a similar article which is free. Of course, until you have paid for an article which is not free, we cannot access it to see if it is, in fact, what is required for a particular piece of work. This is why Google is attempting to digitise a huge proportion of knowledge so you stay on the Google site for longer, thus enabling Google to sell advertising space.

There is no substitute for the occasional inspired contributor, and that is one of the things that makes surfing the internet so attractive. At any moment you may discover something really worthwhile. How else would what is essentially a huge collection of biased information be able to entrance so many people? It's a kind of new 'enlightenment' period. Is the statement 'I read it on the internet' a valid argument? A few months ago, the value of the dollar started to slide. I decided to indulge in some internet based fortune telling and looked online for any indicators I could find. Most financial sites thought that by May 2007, the dollar would have regained its value. In fact this has not happened at all – the dollar broke through the $2.00 to a £1 barrier. So the 'internet' was wrong. Or was I wrong for trusting it?

Information on the internet is rather similar to that found in articles when people write at the bottom 'the views of the author do not reflect those of the BBC/*Guardian*' or whatever organisation they are writing for. It may not be correct, grounded in fact or authorised. It's transient.

It is also inherently unfair. Half the world does not have access to the internet. The UK and US are supposedly ahead of the world in having 80% broadband use; however, in other ways, these developed nations are falling behind. The UK is no longer the manufacturing heart of the world. Not only does the UK not manufacture plastic carrier bags, but it has also devised a way of sending the same, used plastic bags back to China and India for recycling, and the same is true of old computer parts. Noxious fumes and dangerous recovery techniques mean that the developing countries are twice affected by our use of plastic. However, the internet has also contributed to job losses, and these have happened in the developed world, so all is not trouble free in the new online world. The fact that many businesses have decided to operate online means that fewer people are required to man offices. Banks, post offices (why pack up a parcel and take it to a post office when a cheap courier can be booked online, and they come to your premises?), insurance companies, stationery suppliers – all of these can be moved online.

Where the internet ultimately scores is in providing a free shop window to small businesses. If you can book accommodation in small guest houses, buy books direct from small publishers, order organic honey or raspberry vinegar or find rare CDs through the company that recorded them, then we could have an economy in which self-employment becomes the norm. With self-employment comes the freedom to work at a pace which you set for yourself, rather than being slave-driven by a boss – the pyjama work force.

Debate and journalism

The blog has one aspect which is new, although unfortunately we have not yet worked out how to monitor it: the comment. Under most blogs, there is the facility to add a comment. This has two purposes – firstly, it shows the author of the blog that someone is reading, and absorbing your information. It may not be appreciated or agreed with, and indeed comments which are rude and offensive can be blocked, but it does show that you are not just sounding off to yourself. Secondly, the person who has written the comment has a chance to counter what they have just read, instantly and in a location where other people interested in the subject matter can read it. This is a form of democracy.

The following article in *The Economist* 'It's the links, stupid' from April 2006, which is available online at the moment, commented:

> Inadvertently, Mr von Matt had put his finger on something big: that, at least in democratic societies, everybody does have the right to hold opinions, and that the urge to connect and converse with others is so basic that it might as well be added to life, liberty and the pursuit of happiness. 'It's about democratisation, where people can participate by writing back' says Sabeer Bhatia, who in March launched a company called BlogEverywhere.com that lets people

> attach blogs to any web page with a single click. 'Just as everybody has an email account today, everybody will have a blog in five years,' says Mr Bhatia, who helped to make email ubiquitous by starting Hotmail, a web-based email service now owned by Microsoft. This means, Mr Bhatia adds, that 'journalism won't be a sermon any more, it will be a conversation.'

In the future, there is a possibility that political issues will be influenced through the use of a blog and comments. When the congestion charge was being discussed in parliament in Britain, the website promoting it had so many dissenters that the government was forced to abandon its policy, since there was a possibility that normal trade would grind to a halt and the Labour Party would alienate voters. The power of the internet and the ability to vote using a website was cited by the press as a successful use of public opinion to change the course of a government. Other e-petitions on the Downing Street website currently include one to stop the need for a public license to perform music, and one to stop the government regulating the taking of photographs in public places. On the Downing Street website, you have to provide personal details which are verifiable; however, it is possible that like postal voting, such a system would be open to misrepresentation and abuse. It is virtually impossible to check the credentials of all web commentators or verify all email addresses, and one could see the use of the internet as being discounted fairly easily by adverse journalism.

It is possible that right now we are in an internet golden age, when opinions expressed online are still seen as genuine, coming from individuals with their own opinions. In the future, it is possible that the use of specially written software will enable people to swamp websites with biased comments and votes so that the results of these will no longer be trusted. In much the same way as spam means that emails from people you do not know are almost always deleted or ignored and certainly seen as intrusive. Just as email marketing is not as powerful as one would have thought, it follows that judging the response to a website by the comments will be seen as an untrustworthy gauge.

Who is using the internet for what reason?

One of the main attractions of book blogs is that the writer usually has no reason for writing about books other than the fact that they love them. Although publishers will send review copies to book blogs they admire and like, publishers do not send new books to everyone who asks. I doubt that book bloggers start their websites in the hope that a steady stream of free books will come their way. Firstly, reading is a skill that takes both energy and commitment. I doubt many people read more than three books over a very quiet and possibly rainy weekend, or one which is sunny and in which one has access to a secluded garden and a comfortable chair. The last thing you need is a constant diet of books which are chosen by someone other than yourself. The most pleasurable activity a reader can become involved in is browsing in a bookshop or library then going home with four or five books under one's arm, the question of 'in what order to read them' to be debated at leisure. To have to start reading a book because you feel obliged to mention it on your website must take a great deal of the pleasure out of this activity.

Most people do not read more than thirty books a year. However, there are some people in this world who seem to construct websites for other, less altruistic reasons. I had a phone call this week from someone running a website about world affairs who told me he was one of the most influential people in the world and please would I send him a particular book for free. I checked his website saw it was no more than a page of links and deleted his follow up email. It was a prime example of how not to use the internet; his site was a sham and I presume an excuse to bother a lot of people asking for free goods.

A major problem with websites is that it is often impossible to see the organisations behind them. Very few websites contain the names of members of staff, which I find puzzling. What exactly is the point of maintaining a shop window which is virtually free to construct if you then stop people who you wish to attract from contacting you? If I find an e-commerce site which does contain the names of key people, I think the better of the organisation. It's an issue of trust, a degree of transparency makes me more likely to want to do business with a company. If there is just a 'sales@' or 'info@' email address, I can imagine being fobbed off with excuses if something were to go wrong with my transaction, so I am unlikely to progress further with my interest. This is basic psychology – an internet site with no contact names is like a shop where the assistants turn away from you as you enter to start talking amongst themselves. Is a particular site constructed by one person with a clear vision of the information they wish to impart? Or is it owned by a large media organisation and acting as a showcase, as is the way with many newspaper sites? Who decides on the prominence of different parts of a site? Why does the books page always have to be hidden in a section with a grand name, as until recently on the *Independent* website, so that you need to know in advance how to find it?

With the use of professional website designers, it is quite possible for the websites of many different organisations to look incredibly similar, simply because they use the same web design firm. I actually think one of the most liberating aspects of website construction is that the software is comparatively easy to learn and thus it is possible for most organisations to construct and maintain their own websites. I think this is particularly true for small publishing houses which do not have a huge amount of money to give to consultants or to spend on outsourcing necessary services such as accountancy, which is a legal requirement, let alone their website which will need updating on an almost daily basis to be of any use.

Truth and the internet

The nature of truth and the internet is one which is taxing in the extreme. Do you believe everything you read on the internet, in much the same way that you have most likely been taught at school not to trust everything in the newspapers? How do you tell truth from fiction? Who are the people who write websites? It is easy to hide behind an internet persona. In fact, the explosion of social networking sites on the internet is a perfectly acceptable way in which you can massage your public identity, only publishing pictures showing yourself in a favourable light, writing about the esoteric, cool novels you have just read and even including files where people can listen to your own rock music. When the internet is used in politics, though, the repercussions are more serious.

Chad Post is American who was an editor at the excellent Dalkey Archive Press until he moved onto new pastures, and his blog used to be on the World Without Borders website, but is no longer. It is the first case, I think, of content in this book disappearing from the internet due to time passing, changes in life and computers, and website revamps. (See Ms Snark, whose blog was mentioned earlier.) He is a kind of litmus test for the state of world literature and always seems to know what's going on. A year ago he was in New York at PEN World Voices, which is now an annual event bringing some of the best international writers together. It seems that the festival included a talk on the power of the internet and the nature of truth. Any vestige of this talk has probably disappeared in the mists of time (ie two years later) and this is where blogs can be useful, as they can record conversations, and as 'the new correspondence', perhaps one day blog records will come to be published just as collections of letters are today. I think the whole nature of debate on the internet is one which will be with us for a long time and will most likely produce some extremely erudite and detailed books from academic presses – a remit outside the one of this book, which is to highlight some of the best internet practitioners in 2007. However, this is what Chad Post was interested in during PEN World Voices 2006:

> **PEN World Voices: Day Four**
>
> My favorite panel yesterday was on 'Truth and the Internet.' Unfortunately, however, no one came out in favour of lies on the Internet. Really, that's what I'm in favour of. There's no better place to start rumors and create mass hysteria than a website.
>
> George Saunders surprised me by being so anti-blogging and so pro-truth. One would think he'd be into some fun-n-games online, but instead, he claimed that in democracies, the most sane and polished statement is the one that will win out.
>
> That's totally false, in my opinion. The most entertaining, captivating stories always win. Sanity, truth, and artifice, these aren't as valued in today's society as celebrity and glitz.

The internet is an open media and of course websites and emails are closely linked. Every person who has an email account receives a great many unsolicited emails with links to websites and it seems that some people are not able to distinguish truth from rumour mongering. As far back as 1997, CNet.News.com had a feature on truth and the internet, saying:

> People shouldn't believe everything they read – especially, it seems, on the internet. Cyberculture runs rampant with stories about spoofs, virus scares, urban legends, and outright fraud. The fact that a message can circulate from its point of origin or a circle of people to all corners of the worldwide network is the Net's greatest and most garish feature.
>
> Recently, this duality was epitomised by the Kurt Vonnegut email hoax, where a university commencement speech purportedly by the author was in fact a *Chicago Tribune* column written by Mary

Schmich. Thousands, if not more, had a chuckle and forwarded it to others without a thought to its authenticity. While this was a relatively harmless occurrence, one can easily imagine more embarrassing revelations (remember Pierre Salinger's TWA missile theory?), as well as libellous or otherwise damaging consequences to online information.

The TWA missile theory was that a missile from a US Navy ship was responsible for the explosion of TWA Flight 800, although eventually investigators discovered a fuel tank explosion had caused it. However, the report by Pierre Salinger gained such veracity that the term 'Pierre Salinger Syndrome' was coined, meaning a belief that everything on the internet is true. The Pen World Voices discussion included writer Asne Seierstad. When asked whether she used the internet for her writing, she replied that it hardly came into her thought processes.

> 'Not so much. I think I seem to be technologically the most old-fashioned on the panel. I mostly never use the internet. In Afghanistan, where the illiteracy rate is more than 80%, how are you supposed to use the internet? It is the educated world who is able to do that. Why I haven't used the internet? Probably because it doesn't suit me. What I try to achieve in my books is the feeling that the reader has met someone, or something, new. That he or she has learned something about a different society from where they live in.
>
> You can get a lot of important information on the internet but you might not get as much knowledge. I think that's what you can get through books. You're sitting in a different way, maybe in a good chair and you're not looking at a screen. You can interact in a different way with a book and perhaps what we need in our society is not overwhelming information but compassionate understanding. I'm interested in going somewhere, sitting on a dirty floor and waiting for people

> to speak, not rushing, but just getting their story. That is a face-to-face thing, not something you can do through email or internet.

In the same talk, Asne Seierstad referred to Riverbend of *Baghdad Burning*. The importance of Riverbend was that she was not a Western reporter, as Asne is. Her reports on Iraq, which could only be disseminated on the internet, had an accuracy that a visiting reporter could not achieve. And yet, it was only when collected into a book, first by The Feminist Press in New York and then when we followed by publishing her blogs in the UK that she became noticed and began to be regarded as a true voice from Iraq. While publishing Riverbend's blogs, the main issue I have had to tackle is whether she actually exists. For Asne, the quality of her writing means that she does not question this. Riverbend has to stay anonymous for her safety, but right at the beginning she did give this publishing house a few clear details about her life which have been verified. However, they remain confidential, and thus the debate on truth and the internet is one in which her blog name will be raised many times over the coming years.

For many years, artificial intelligence and the growth of machines taking over human functions has been firmly kept in the domain of science fiction. In the internet age, unless people can trust the sources of information found on the internet, we will become a race hoodwinked and seduced by the ease of information. Wikipedia is a wonderful thing but we know that it cannot be relied upon as an accurate source for academic use since the articles on it are submitted by enthusiasts and there are few checks.

One of the main obstacles that lies between truth and the internet is the fact that information on the web is free at the point of consumption. Everything you read on the internet is there for the taking. The concept of a 'creative commons' license or 'copyleft' is one that independent presses do not have a huge problem with, since they can see the merits of using the web as a disseminator of ideas. When it comes to reading a book, there is no good substitute for paper and ink, because your eyes tire, and the computer has limited portability. Computers also suffer technical problems, and the odd crack in a book's binding is a small problem compared with the discovery that your internet settings have somehow vanished into thin air.

The point at which this publisher's generosity in encouraging authors who have websites to post their work disappears is when confronted with the large internet corporations who are greedy for the content of every single provider. Google wishes to make available the content of all books online, claiming that this will lead to more book sales. For academic books, this is clearly nonsense, since students are poor and fairly lazy and would far prefer to do all their research online rather than having to visit a library or buy a book. If the content is not available for free online, they will just have to invest in books. In fact, I would argue that one of the main benefits of a degree is to have keepsakes in the form of a library of books, albeit ones you have scribbled in the margins of. This means that twenty years later, when you wish to remind yourself what Wittgenstein's *Tractatus Logico-Philosphicus* actually said, you can pick up your old student copy and see at a glance what you thought then. Memory is a fickle and short-lived thing and if you didn't have this store of books, you would surely soon forget.

However, my main objection to the Google digitisation process is that the company did not wish to pay for the books that they scanned. They offered to pay for the transportation, but they declined to give back to the publisher a print quality PDF file of the book. At the time they started their campaign, around 2003, it cost around £250 to digitise a book. This has now fallen to around £80 which is absorbable by a small press. In 2003, to have had our backlist, all set many years before desktop publishing, would have been an incentive to join Google's scheme, allowing them to scan our books and make available small extracts for free on Google's site. Looking back on the decision not to join, and seeing how Murdoch and Google are swallowing every internet company in sight, and becoming huge organisations, I think I made the right decision.

The importance of Google in the search for information and truth is crucial. It is the favourite search engine by far, and almost everyone who uses the internet on a regular basis will thus interact with Google every day. The company is unique in both the way that it operates and how it courts public opinion. The Managing Director of Google, Eric Schmidt, addressed the Conservative Party conference in October 2006, warning politicians that soon there would be a widget on Google which would be able to compare a politician's statement to every piece of historical evidence on the subject and thus work out whether or not the politician was lying. So the debate about global warning would be assisted by the evidence of the Google tool, since the widget would tell you whether the planet was about to disappear under water or suffer from a major drought – just two of the opposing arguments commentators were laying before us in 2007, a few weeks before much of England was devastated by floods while we still had intact memories of the stifling heat and drought of the summer of 2006. In essence, the widget would be able to gather information from internet sources all over the world and thus have more useful intelligence than the commentatators on drought and flood, since it would have more evidence of the likelihood of one over the other. Google was able to send their director to address the Conservative party, and get the party to listen, since Google represents the future and commercialism. Eric Schmidt's point was that elections in the future would be run on the internet, with analysis provided by Google, a company which claims to be apolitical. I find it hard to see how a company which is aiming for internet domination in every country, will not be in league with the political party which governs each country's stock market, investment and tax law.

The Google example shows what might seem an unimportant issue, the intent to digitise intellectual content no matter to whom it belongs, could easily grow into a very dangerous ability for one company to control how information on the internet is made available. We have already seen the censorship in China of Google, with many sites blocked from appearing and it is plain that Google must know of this and have had conversations with the Chinese government. It is quite sad that the same force that is seen as an opening up of information could find itself prey to the control of one or two huge corporations.

Catheryn Kilgarriff

Dissidents and Rebels: Bloggers who Publish

For some book bloggers, writing about the publishing ventures of others just doesn't go far enough in terms of swaying the literary tastes of the masses. These people have radical opinions about the state of the publishing industry and are not afraid to a) air them, b) transfer their disaffection into action. Disappointed with the predictable fare they claim the major houses are releasing, these self-proclaimed saviours of experimental literature are using the internet as a way to publish work – branded not-sellable – that cannot reach readers otherwise because no-one will take it on.

Using the internet as a tool for self-publishing in the way that print journals and zines have always operated in the past, this is 'literature for the MySpace generation' as the *Guardian* call it: in-your-face online publishing that is intended to leap off the screen. Lee Rourke from *Scarecrow* magazine – which is very much a part of the UK underground publishing scene – sums up the attitude of himself and his peers.

> This gathering of like-minded individuals who all eschew the current trend in publishing, have acted alone. We are elsewhere. We don't belong. We have, more or less, turned our backs on the conglomerates; we ignore those vainglorious money-men who'd rather lunch in the stinking, laughable Groucho than sniff out new writing talent; those moronic cretins hell-bent on sales, sales, sales; we ignore marketing departments; those same bozos responsible

> for the horrid 3-for-2 dross in every high street bookstore; those grand panjandrums that are mostly responsible for everything that is wrong with contemporary literary fiction in this country...'

Like Rourke says, there are a variety of book bloggers who feel the same and their sphere of activity is growing. But do these people really need to set themselves 'against' the rest of the publishing industry? And is this, in fact, what they actually do?

Literature for the MySpace generation

Writing about bloggers who publish, Sam Jordison notes in the *Guardian* recently (February 2007) that, '...if they continue to expand their influence as rapidly as they have been doing in recent months, mainstream publishers will have to sit up and take serious notice,' but in fact this is already happening. With some of the better known independents already beginning to publish work that has been championed by these self-proclaimed dissidents it is perhaps only a matter of time before the larger houses follow. SnowBooks have, for example, published *3:AM* Magazine's anthology *Edgier Waters* in 2006. Canongate label this website 'brilliant, gutsy' and 'one of the best litzines on the net' and Serpent's Tail sing its praises also: 'one of the best arts magazines on the net'. Chosen by author Adele Stripe as her best literary website for 2006 in ISSUE 16 of www.laurahird.com (Winter 2007) and included also in *Time Out*'s 'Best Book Blogs' round-up in February 2007, by all accounts *3:AM* Magazine fulfils its promise of proving to be a 'dip into edgier waters'.

An early pioneer

Founded in April 2000 by Andrew Gallix, in the wake of book blogs Salon.com and Nerve, *3:AM* and its associated blog Buzzwords is one of the oldest litblogs in the world. Conceived of as an extension of publishing traditions begun by the likes of Rebel Inc and Between C & D, the magazine matches a post-punk outlook with an emphasis on 'blank generation' authors. Buzzwords, the blog, is written by a combination of editors and reviewers including Andrew Stevens and Ellen Kennedy, as well as Gallix himself of course. The point is to publish work online and in print that wouldn't get a look in elsewhere. So alongside the reviews, interviews and features that other book blogs might include, you also get new fiction and short stories from unpublished authors, and they even publish the odd book or two, again largely anthologies of the magazine's favourite authors.

Writing for *The Times* in 2001, just one year after the launch of the website, Bill Broun made it clear that *3:AM* had already won fans in the mainstream press:

> The cosmopolitan, *rive gauche* quality of the site is wonderfully obvious. From 'cutting edge short fiction' to political satire and music reviews, *3:AM* is a dream publication for the young, literary and clued-up, and it counter-balances nicely the London/New York publishing behemoth.

And this initially enthusiastic reception has no means dulled over the years. In *The Scotsman* in June 2006 for example, we are told that:

> The editors of *3:AM* know that dissent has become a commodity in our culture. They realise that young artistic tyros will Bush-bash to build a name and get a fat book deal, then move uptown and start drinking chilled dry whites. By contrast, the writers here are published online or underground; they make little money, and best of all, they don't seem to care about their 'careers'. This is literature as it should be – free, sometimes too free, from editorial control, frank and outrageous.'

Even punk legend Richard Hell is jumping on the bandwagon

to declare his allegiance, declaring on his own website (www.richardhell.com, March 2006) that: 'I get my buzz at *3:AM*'

What Makes *3:AM* different?

So what exactly does the website include? Diverse enough to include comments from stalwart writers of the 'underground' scene – see Tom McCarthy on Bataille ('He chops a man's head off, makes the sun bleed and the sky reek with the stench of God's decomposing flesh. When I become Minister of Culture, his pornographic masterpiece *Story of the Eye* will be the first book on the National Curriculum') – this site also features relative newcomers like the twenty-three-year-old Brooklyn-based Tao Lin.

'A reader of Depressing Books,' Tao Lin is an author who blogs, an editor for *3:AM* and counts amongst those new writers who are already making a name for themselves through their online literary pursuits. In a recent interview with *Time Out New York* conducted in an East Village coffee shop, Lin announces in his typically flippant manner: 'Now I try not to think in terms of happiness or depression – I just think in terms of whether I'm productive or not.' And Lin is nothing if not prolific, with a book of poetry under his belt already, his first novel *Eeeee Eee Eeee* has just been published, as well as collection of short stories called *Bed*.

Of course, *3:AM* isn't just about literature, it counts amongst those book blogs that also include comments from rock stars (see 'new ravers' The Klaxons comments on crowd surfers) fashion designers (Vivienne Westwood, 'Descartes is shit!' declares punk's first lady as she sends up conceptual art in her anti-philistine manifesto at the Hay Festival this year) and politicians. The idea is to place literature within a scene. It has its place amongst the artistic, musical and otherwise creative pursuits which dominate the UK and US subculture. The important thing is that these art forms share the same ideals and aspirations. It's not what you're doing but how and why you do it that counts.

For an example of *3:AM*'s book reviews see Andrew Steven's review of Philippe Vasset's highly innovative *ScriptGenerator©®™* for *3:AM*, a novel which explores the possibility of dispensing with the author altogether. Stevens begins with a quick plot summary:

> *ScriptGenerator©®™* is perfectly observed and a stunning indictment of contemporary cultural production values. The computer programme of the book's title treats the narrative assembly process as just the same as any other, a string of variables just waiting to be arranged. Therefore the discovery of such a programme spells the end of the creative profession for good, rendering writers entirely redundant. Anyone who's witnessed people in public places glued to Dan Brown's *Da Vinci Code* can only wonder if this is such a bad thing?

Before progressing to contemplate the consequences of the mythical 'ScriptGenerator' and offering an appraisal of this 'bold and daring' novel:

> The ability to dispense with writers altogether must represent something of a juicy prospect for most publishing houses. No more egos to contend with. No more manuscripts to wade through. No more PR hassles. And most importantly, no royalty cheques to issue. Philippe Vasset's debut teasingly guides us to such an imprint utopia but raises important questions in the process. The commodification of culture is, for all intents and purposes, the third oldest profession but in recent times has accelerated by several mach. Literature itself cannot deem itself to be insulated from such trends, whether they be the whims of marketing departments or the altogether unnecessary 'Lit Idol'. The denial of writing as a craft has manifested itself with vacuous

> celebrities from the worlds of acting, singing and modelling seeking to purge themselves of some inner book or other that really shouldn't be foisted onto an already over-crowded market for tepid bullshit by vacuous people.
>
> Vasset's[...]has presented us with a paradox whereby the novel on offer is bold and daring enough to taunt critics yet has, by and large, attracted praise across the board for this. *The ScriptGenerator*©®™ programme's 'Zeitgeist Index' (where writing themes are tested for contemporary relevance) is probably already in production somewhere, if it wasn't then it is now. Vasset can certainly look to a place among the eager crop of younger French (if not European) novelists who are more willing to defy genre and put society on trial and allow us to marvel at the results. The only let-down of the novel is its compact size in length, Vasset could have easily stretched the concept a little further (a Sunday newspaper might preoccupy you longer). But innovative fiction has enough David Foster Wallaces on its books.

But if writers are on their way out according to this plot, then reviewers can surely not be much further behind?

Social Disease

Thirty-three-year-old, London-based Heidi James has followed in the footsteps of *3:AM* to create a publishing venture that is very much her own and very much in opposition to the domination of the industry by the regular reviewers, booksellers, publishers, authors.

Social Disease (socialdisease.wordpress.com) is a one woman operation that functions as a book blog, a print-on-demand online publisher and in recent years, an 'ordinary' publisher selling also from mainstream outlets. The idea is that by utilising new technology, especially the internet, for scouting and print-on-demand services offered recently by various major printers, the outlet can operate beyond the constraints of marketing budgets, profit margins and booksellers' dictates and release literature that is bold, innovative and experimental. Of course, there is always the problem with print-on-demand that if the publicity isn't gained for an operation or particular title, no-one will know to seek it out. But this is true of all publishing, so James needn't be daunted by the challenge any more than anyone else.

Heidi James explains her motivation in an interview for the *Guardian* (February 2007):

> Zadie Smith is not fucking interesting. All this postmodern irony is just so dull. And I realised that I really hate the homogeneity of the publishing world where it's next to impossible to get genuinely interesting work published. The big publishing houses would have you believe that there isn't a market for new and exciting work that takes a few risks and makes a demand on its readers, but that's bollocks. Absolute bollocks.'

To counteract this perceived blandness in mainstream publishing she aims to publish work that will challenge readers, taking her company name from the infamous Andy Warhol quote:

> I have Social Disease. I have to go out every night. If I stay home one night I start spreading rumours to my dogs.

Social Disease is a prime example of 'literature for the MySpace generation'. For anyone who is yet to familiarise themselves with this phenomena, MySpace is an online community originally intended for musicians to share information about bands/gigs/new releases etc but also intended as a place to make new friends, a forum for discussion and a platform to promote the music itself. So you can download the songs of any band who is willing to donate them for free and look at photos of all your favourite musicians, whilst forming networks via a system of approving people as 'friends'.

Since its conception, and perhaps due to the emphasis on music (with the likes of Lily Allen showcasing the possibilities that the site might offer someone trying to crack the industry) the number of MySpace users has rocketed into phenomenally high figures – and spawned a string of imitators such as Facebook. The site was started by the multi-million-dollar corporation eUniverse (not student-types Tom Anderson and Chris deWolfe as News Corp, who now own the enterprise, would have us all believe). As nineteen-year-old-journalism student and blogger Trent Lapinski writes on the scandalous story of the MySpace con:

> Both the *New York* and the *Los Angeles Times* got it wrong. MySpace isn't the brainchild of DeWolfe or Anderson, this was a Wiederhorn job. DeWolfe and Anderson were mere cabin-boys… The site was created by a multimillion dollar company then purchased by a multibillion dollar entertainment/news company (Fox, News Corp.). The site was not a garage project; MySpace was created and coded by people being paid considerable salaries sitting in an office building in Los Angeles.

The story of its faked origins is scandalous indeed. But the point at this juncture is that the outfit is proving hugely successful and its popularity is growing daily. With one branch focusing on music networking, and another intended to service individuals who are not necessarily interested in music but are keen to form online friendships, the number of MySpace users has rocketed since its conception. And catching onto its success – recognising the potential in terms of reaching new audiences – there are a growing numbers of artists, writers and musicians logging on and signing up also. You only have to look at the number of 'friends' Social Disease has immediate access to realise that online publishing can benefit hugely from having a ready made market and the means to keep in contact with it on a daily basis.

Social Disease has in fact been enjoying a significant amount of attention from 'real' booksellers and James now has the pleasure of seeing the independents stock titles she has selected herself. But even if they weren't, her books can be bought through Amazon or direct from her website. With no start-up costs, no overheads, and no huge advances to pay (the authors are paid in royalties alone), the beauty of this kind of operation is that the focus really is on the promotion of new talent. Money-making is not the object – and would in fact be difficult seeing as print-on-demand keeps unit costs extremely high (the unit cost of a print run for just one book is the same as for 10,000 books.)

Examples of the extreme-sounding titles she publishes include *The Swank Bisexual Wine Bar of Modernity* by HP Tinker and *Seizure Wet Dreams* by Tony O'Neil, both of which seem to fit the remit she announces on the MySpace site:

> Established as an antidote to publishers who slavishly pander to so-called market forces and therefore rejecting great books as a corollary, Social Disease began as a monthly Literary Mini-zine publishing incredible short stories.
>
> Our aim is to publish extraordinary literature regardless of its pedigree or 'niche' in the market or indeed lack of.
>
> You want to read challenging and beautiful literature. We want to publish it.

Of course James's venture is not the only one of this ilk. Lee Rourke of *Scarecrow Magazine* was quoted earlier in this chapter, but it's worth taking a closer look at the work he has been producing. A thirty-something Mancunian currently residing in London's trendiest hotspot, the newly glamourised Hackney, Rourke is the founder and editor of this forward-thinking publication.

Against 'bookish blatherites'

Scarecrow was founded in October 2004 as an online forum for book reviews, literary comment, short fiction and nationwide art when, quite disillusioned with events in the publishing world, Rourke decided to turn his back on the mainstream 'bookish blatherskites' and focus primarily on misunderstood, ignored and abandoned underground and independent literary fiction and culture. The editorial on his home page (www.hodmandod.blogspot.com) tries to tempt new readers in with the promise of a burgeoning literary scene:

> If you'd have asked me one year ago if a literary scene existed and was alive and most definitely kicking in London, or New York, or California... anywhere, I'd have laughed at the very thought. We're still standing in that long, drawn out shadow The Beats created I would have wailed. I would have bemoaned the very nature of it (not that there is anything wrong with The Beats really – I mean, has anyone actually touched the genius of William S Burroughs since? I very much doubt it). But now, one year on, ask me. Go on, ask me...

For according to Lee Rourke, the new scene is here, and he is very much a part of it:

> Well, it's already happened. I think. And it seems to have happened right under our noses. And we've created it. It was our design. Not a marketing team in sight. We stand alone.

The blurb on the MySpace page announces that:

> *Scarecrow* continues to bang the drum for the unheard, the unconventional, the eccentric, the revolutionary and the radical, and has evolved into a showcase for published and unpublished writers

> of short fiction and poetry and receives submissions from all corners of the globe each week – some make its pages, most don't.

So DIY publishing isn't necessarily all-embracing. Once again the remit to potential authors is clear – *Scarecrow* is interested in ballsy, experimental writing. Indeed, half-an-hour's browsing on the MySpace pages reveals quickly that the same names will crop up again and again here. Scarecrow publishes authors such as Stewart Home, Tom McCarthy, Tony O'Neill, Paul Ewen, Ellis Sharp, HP Tinker, Mark SaFranko, Robert Woodard, for example, but as we've seen, Social Disease also publishes Tony O'Neill and HP Tinker. The various players on this particular underground scene are all supportive of each other, and though they welcome newcomers I wonder whether many might find these people intimidating, such is their aggressive determination to be 'different'.

Naming Wrecking Ball Press of Hull as a like-minded outfit, alongside Burning Shore Press in the US, *Scarecrow* offers interviews, reviews, short fiction, 'poetics', essays and art alongside the book reviews and other book related posts. His latest being 'What are you reading?' and 'The joys of academic books.' Here's a quick sample from his recent review of Anna Kavan's latest novel *Guilty* published by Peter Owen after a lost manuscript turned up out of the blue at the University of Tulsa:

> I, for one, am deliriously happy about the publication of *Guilty,* since Anna Kavan, who died in 1968, is one our greatest and most original novelists.
>
> Born in 1901, she is perhaps the only novelist ever to have taken on the name of one of her characters... Legally adopting the name of the protagonist in her third novel, *Let Me Alone,* she made her intentions more than clear. It seemed that Anna Kavan wanted to retreat away from the world around her. It seemed that she, in fact, wanted to fictionalise herself - she even destroyed almost all her

journals and personal diaries before her death. ...

But, like most writers, it's her work that interests me, not her life...Anna Kavan's writing is a surrealist fictionalisation of her own mental breakdown; she charts every pulse-bleep of despair. Ironically her writing is about as real as it gets...it is the great writers, it seems, who realise this; it is the great writers who understand that not only do they have to produce original works, they have to embody them wholly too.

Like most posthumously published novels *Guilty* probably will not be Anna Kavan's greatest work but it is still eagerly awaited. It is slowly becoming apparent that Anna Kavan actually matters (as Doris Lessing will testify). Her work has stood the test of time because it transcends mere voice: it is a state of mind. A solipsistic retreat that openly contradicts itself, it invites us closer to its centre. And although Anna Kavan didn't want her readers to be concerned with superfluous stuff like the scraps of biography writers leave behind, we get a pure shot of her own reality through her work despite how surreal and cold it may seem on the surface.

This new publication is a timely reminder that most debut novels today don't break new ground and it is down to great British writers such as Anna Kavan – in these crass, commercial, sanitised times – to restore my true faith in literature.

Lee Rourke also reviews books for www.readysteadybook.com. His short fiction has been published in numerous online and print publications and he regularly writes for *Dazed and Confused's* online edition (www.dazedigital.com) and London's *The Penny.* His collection of stories are to be published through Social Disease in early 2007.

Rebecca Gillieron

Riot Lit and the Literary Groups Who Blog

BritLit and other angry bloggers en masse

There is a new movement in town. We've had BritArt, we've had Brit Pop and now there is BritLit. A term adopted by many but justified by few, it is loosely taken to refer to the young, new literature that is emerging in the capital, across the suburbs, the nation and beyond. But what's this got to do with book blogging? Many of the groups that are forming under the wide umbrella of this uninformative term are blogging *en masse*. Too busy to run a site as individuals, or just preferring to do so with like-minded souls, these literary groups are taking on the business of promoting their work as a unit, and promoting their preferred style of literature as a whole. Be warned...

The Brutalists

The Brutalists is a literary group formed by writers Tony O'Neill, Adelle Stripe and Ben Myers in 2006 via MySpace – perhaps the first literary groups to use this medium as a launch pad. Though Stripe runs a weblog titled 'Straight From the Fridge' and Ben Myers' first novel *The Book of Fuck* has been likened to the work of Charles Bukowski and Hunter S Thomspon, Tony O'Neill seems to have the most fiction in print (Myers also writes non-fictional works on rock musicians with a distinctly punk aesthetic).

A New York-based musician and author who has played with the likes of indie band Kenickie, as well as Ex-Soft Cell frontman Marc Almond, O'Neill's autobiographical novel *Digging the Vein* was well received in Canada and the US (Dan Fante, son of John Fante, is said to be a fan) and his collection of short stories titled *Seizure Wet Dreams* was published by the aforementioned Social Disease in 2006. (It quickly becomes clear that the new BritLit scene is more than a little incestuous…)

On their MySpace page The Brutalists claim that 'Brutalist writing is open to anyone who shares similar ideals about the role of literature,' and whilst they do not spell out the nature of this role, it is perfectly clear what these ideals involve. The Brutalists see themselves as a band who have 'put down their instruments and picked up their pens and scalpels instead.'

Borrowing Mark Perry's infamous call to arms as featured in the punk zine *Sniffin Glue* – 'Here's a chord. Here's another one. Here's another one. Now form a band!' that inspired so many wanna-be punks to get playing way back in the 1970s – the group incite writers with their bastardised version of the now legendary slogan:

> Here's a laptop, here's the spell check, now write a book.

But this isn't just about having fun. The intention behind the movement is deadly serious.

> Brutalism calls for writing that touches upon levels of raw honesty that is a lacking from most mainstream fiction. We cannot simply sit around waiting to be discovered – we would rather do it ourselves. Total control, total creativity.'

As with many online literary activists, these people are not satisfied with contemporary literature and refuse to accept the situation as they see it. It is refreshing to hear about such impassioned and motivated individuals. As they declare:

> Brutalism is an ideology born out of frustration and surplus energy, the writers involved united by various factors: we are all approx thirty years old or under from small Northern towns but living in cities (Tony in NY, Ben and Adelle in London). In our past, none of us have been strangers to narcotics abuse, seedy sex, and transatlantic travel. Tony has been in successful pop bands, Ben a known music journalist/record label owner and Adelle a promoter, performance poet and band manager.
>
> We draw inspiration from music (punk, post-punk, jazz, hardcore, thrash metal) as much as we do literature. We're fans of Dan Fante, Herbert Huncke, and Billy Childish, though we are not attempting imitate or emulate anyone. We are also united by our disgust with mainstream publishing world that consistently rejects us; now we no longer care. 'Brutalism' means writing that shows no quarter. Writing that rages and burns across the page – writing that doesn't worry about causing offence, breaking taboos, cutting to the heart of it Writing that may shock and shake the reader into submission rather than gently caress them. We're not anti-intellectual or anti-literary but we are anti-apathy and we exist in a highly agitated state.
>
> Crucially though, the Brutalists are not born out of bitterness – we have had already had acclaimed debut novels published through independent publishers and in different languages... We met and continue to publish much of our work online, where publishing is democratised and the author can exert greater control over their work. For better for worse we are the first wave of internet writers and have had our work published on dozens of sites.
>
> That said, between us we have numerous stories and poems coming out in 2007 in various books, for various publishers – Social Disease, Serpent's Tail etc. We are also formally launching Brutalism with a limited edition collection of poems by the

three of us, scheduled for publication early 2007. It will be called BRUTALISM #1 and will feature five poems by each of us, based around our hometowns of Blackburn, Tadcaster and Durham. It will be the first in a series, publishing like-minded writers. BRUTALISM #2 will follow shortly afterwards.

No one could accuse these people of being apathetic. However, not everyone is a fan. On the *3:AM* website for example, there was a recent post from someone called Glen Crawford who is not afraid to air his views by way of a poem, mimicking their style:

The Brutalists are angry
And they want you to share their pain
Share their prose
And stick it up your arse
You boring c**t

Judge for yourself. Adelle Stripe's blog Straight From the Fridge claims to solve all your poetry needs (see www.upbondageupyours.blogspot.com) and bring you the very best in Brutalism from across the country. The net is cast wide to include musicians, artists and even flash fiction artists, alongside authors and poets. Stripe writes that 'in particular we are seeking honest writing from the heart, no frills, only flick knives.' Judging by the email address – upbondageupyours@hotmail.co.uk – Straight from the Fridge is a sharp-edged as its associates. Celebrating two years as a print publication and one year on the web (at the time of writing - July 2007) it looks set to continue as one of London's newest showcases for edgy literary talent. Look out also for performance poetry nights, parties and readings from this collective as shows are notoriously sensationalist, extreme and challenging. Though not to everyone's taste.

The Offbeat Generation

The Offbeat Generation is another group writers who are opposed to marketing departments' hold on mainstream publishing houses. Likened to The Brutalists by Sam Jordison in his article 'Surfing the New Literary Wave' (See the *Guardian* February 12th 2007) – whom he labels their 'more sweary cousins' – this group includes authors such as HP Tinker, Paul Ewen and Matthew Coleman alongside increasingly familiar names of this online 'underground' scene like Heidi James, Ben Myers and Tony O'Neill. In fact, *The Offbeat Generation* is the title of a collection of short stories, edited by Matthew Coleman and Andrew Gallix (remember *3:AM*) to be published by Social Disease – so again you can get an idea of how incestuous this scene is. But is this necessarily a bad thing? These people are networking, performing, djing, writing with the intention of shaking up the literary scene. Creating an alternative to the bestsellers lists that dominate the industry. What's there to complain about in that?

N+1 Magazine and the US contingent

There are many other UK based literary groups that blog, but what of the US contingent? Is there a rival emergent scene that sounds the trumpet for young and experimental writers struggling to get their work 'out there'? Yes and it's as vibrant as its UK counterpart.

N+1 magazine, though not strictly a 'group' is one of the better known platforms for new edgy writing in the US, consisting in a twice-yearly print journal as well as posts of new web-only material once or twice a week. With the focus on 'politics, literature and culture' and based in New York this is edited by a team including Keith Gessen, Mark Greif, Chad Harbach, Benjamin Kunkel, Allison Lorentzen and Marco Roth, which, whilst it hardly allows the female contingent much input, at least ensures a broad range of perspectives – and this is not to mention the twenty-or-so other staff they list on the website, catering for all their design needs, publicity, advertising and so forth. This is a major operation.

As a sample of the rather dry, cynical but admittedly quite funny type of posts that are favoured by *N+1* here's a piece (available in the print journal as well as online) about literary readings – which I think are quite enjoyable, but they do have a few points.

Cancel Them
From Issue Two, Part Three of The Intellectual Situation: A Diary

If you've made the mistake of going to literary readings, you know that the only thing that can make them endurable is to *ha* at each funny bit, and *ah* at each clever observation, and oh at any grotesque turn. Pity rescues art on these occasions. But art can't survive it.

A reading is like a bedside visit. The audience extends a giant moist hand and strokes the poor reader's hair. Up at the podium is someone who means to believe in his or her work, and instead he's betrayed by his twitchy body and nervous laughter. The writer looks like his mother dresses him, he has razor burn on his neck, his hands may be shaking, his voice is creaky. Or she – she was always afraid of public speaking, this is why she became a writer!

And so, to send out a little life preserver, you laugh at a line, which maybe wasn't intended to be a joke. The writer looks up, a smile possesses one side of his mouth. He is funny? Tears well up in his eyes. You've saved him. Literature is so much easier than he thought. But one of your laughs, in pity, leads to two, soon people are laughing for no reason. And the work he's reading – well, in this format, who can tell if it's any good on the page? Nobody. And suddenly it's his life we're talking about – not only the words and lines, but the pathetic effort he's devoted his entire life to. This figure in front of you was formerly an independent artist, with at least the solitary belief in himself that a writer needs. Now he's desperate for a laugh.

On the page, the same person can be a sovereign. And you also are sovereign, throwing the book across the room if it's terrible, or paying silent homage if it's brilliant, laughing or crying only when you're moved. Two sovereigns, writer and reader, meet in a nowhere place, proud, independent, and for once in their lives completely undeceitful.

For the reader in his chair, the act of private reading requires forgetting that the person who produced this work of art is a person with a face. The author's physical existence in the mind of a reader is a sign of the writer's failure to do what writing properly does, that is, to create a different world of appearances, one that makes this world so inferior that you don't want to recall yourself to it. You can measure the unsuccess of many a novel by the number of times you turn to the author photo in the back...

The only really justifiable public appearances are by those who are already famous enough to be monuments, their personas set in stone, whose work we love beyond reason because it is so great and strange. Then it's necessary that they appear before readers, so they can confirm that it was a human being who wrote so well, and not a god.

Still, it would be nice for authors simply to step through the doorway – not read – and answer the perennial questions: How do you get your ideas? Where do you write? Do you use a computer? And, unspoken: Do you really exist? Let them sign the book, to prove a human hand wrote the rest. Let that be the end of it.

McSweeney's

Nicknamed 'the daddy of all online magazines' by the *Guardian*, *McSweeney's* was one of the first of the 'edgy' US magazines that has since established a strong online presence, including a much-loved online bookstore and book club. Associated with the Eggersards – a movement of significantly outlandish and avant-garde work spearheaded by Dave Eggers – according to the *Guardian:*

> 'It now has as many detractors as loyal readers, but still seems to have the edge on young pretenders, the particularly user-hostile Underground Literary Alliance and the smart *N+1* magazine.'

The editors at *N+1* also give credit where due, in a post entitled 'a regressive avant-garde' they comment on the Eggersards' impact on the underground literary scene:

> Their journals and readings have staged the most commanding popular art-provocations of the last ten years...
>
> Eggersards created an identifiable style...Eggers proved himself a possibly significant writer. His genius for creating institutions of a less elitist literary culture (*McSweeney's, McSweeney's Books, The Believer)* is beyond question. And if his group restarts the engine of literary innovation and strife, then it will have performed a real historic service.

Before examining what they deem to be the Eggersards' childlike approach and quite deliberate naivety, which they believe to have been a defining characteristic and also the secret of their group's success:

> Eggersards returned to the claims of childhood. Transcendence would not figure in their thought. Intellect did not interest them, but kids did. Childhood is still their leitmotif.'

Although grateful for inspiration from Eggers, three of the group – Heidi Julavatis, Ed Park and Vendela Vida – decided to steer away from his influence and begin their own publication. Reminiscent of *MAD* magazine, *The Believer* was conceived of as an antidote to mainstream criticism and it's 'snarkisness' (I wonder if blogger Ms Snark takes a cue from this?). The idea is that to believe is to be against thinking, against the snobbery of the intellect and in favour of more childlike responses. So the initial issues of the magazine featured 'child' and 'philosopher' who would teach a truth to *The Believer*. Available in print, and purchased through the McSweeney's online store, the manifesto and all encompassing positivity of *The Believer* is declared on their website (see www.believermag.com):

> *The Believer* is a monthly magazine where length is no object. There are book reviews that are not necessarily timely, and that are very often very long. There are interviews that are also very long.
>
> We will focus on writers and books we like.
> We will give people and books the benefit of the doubt.
> The working title of this magazine was *The Optimist*.

But the magazine also functions as a bookstore (a subdivision of McSweeney's) and places a welcome emphasis on translated works:

> Believer Books will seek to introduce readers to titles from around the non-English-speaking world – places like Sweden, Portugal, and Madagascar – translated and published in English for the first time. These jacketed paperbacks will feature a recognisable and cohesive style, and will be affordably priced.

If we are looking for an example of online book reviewers that aren't of the 'inflated ego' type, I would suggest that this collective is a good example. How can you argue with such a simple and self-evident aim of introducing readers to new works in translation by providing them with cheap, presentable books? Recommendations in the July 2007 issue include: *Voyage Along the Horizon* by Javier

Marías, an homage to the great adventure tales of the 19th century, HP Lovecraft's *Against the World, Against Life* and Nick Hornby's virtual-in print-book-blog *The Polysyllabic Spree,* a short extract of the review for the latter is included here:

> Nick Hornby ably explores everything from the classic to the graphic novel, as well as poems, plays, and sports-related exposés. If he occasionally implores a biographer for brevity, or abandons a literary work in favour of an Arsenal soccer match, then all is not lost. His warm and riotous writing, full of all the joy and surprise and despair that books bring him, reveals why we still read, even when there's soccer on TV, a pram in the hall, and a good band playing at our local bar.

See *The Believer Book of Writers Talking to Writers* for a sample of authors that *The Believer* will wholeheartedly support (this features well-respected writers who are mentoring younger authors) from Tobias Wolff, George Saunders, Paul Auster, Janet Malcolm and Jamaica Kincaid.

The Underground Literary Alliance

Featuring a photograph of a gunman wearing a luminous pink balaclava and pointing a gun at the head of some defenceless toy pigs, the Underground Literary Alliance were never going to be run-of-the-mill. But neither are they crazy for crazy's sake. Established by six original members (Karl 'King' Wenclas, Steve Kostecke, Michael Jackman, Ann Sterzinger, Joe Smith and Doug Bassett) and emerging from the zine scene of the 1990s the Philadelphia-based ULA class themselves as outsiders, hosting open mic nights, readings and protests against institutionalised literature. Whereas they once interrupted readings to take on literary stars (they call them 'demi-puppets'), encouraging a 'read-off' between their own writers and whoever else might take the challenge up, they now spread the word via a daily blog and well managed website – with brightly-coloured retro graphics, a punkish looking street-aesthetic and the promise of fireworks:

> If Dave Eggers is koolaid,
> and Rick Moody is milk,
> then we're the literary
> equivalent of booze!

As a sort of self-elected publicity manager and spokesman, King (Karl) Wenclas explains that the ULA was always intended as a PR campaign for good underground writers, operating under the belief that if they spend their time pointing out the shortcomings of established authors this will help the case for the neglected talent. In an interview featured on the listings site CURRENT he outlines the group's ethos:

> We want people to know about them (underground writers). We're the only hope for dying literature in this country – to make the underground mainstream.

Some may question the authority of the ULA, arguing that they've no right to go around attacking others' work and asking whether this method really gets them anywhere, in terms of promoting new writing? I'd make an analogy with an art movement called The Stuckists in the UK which includes a variety of work, some of which is pretty good, with a welcome focus on painting but when their whole *raison d'etre* is to be 'AGAINST' established art practices, against the rise of conceptualism and the institutionalisation of the art world through awards like the Turner Prize, this does make you wonder whether all this energy would be better directed towards the production of something positive. Admittedly, The Stuckists, who exhibit regularly, are far from sitting on their laurels when it comes to putting on shows, maintaining a high profile in the press, promoting new painters, etc., and the same can be said of the ULA, I'm sure, but is the resident vitriol that is ever-present in interviews, on press releases and associated publicity material, really going to achieve anything?

I'm of the opinion that it's worth a go! Apart from anything else, you can't just sit back and NOT say or do anything in situations where you strongly object to a perceived down-turn in artistic merit, whether it is music, art or, in this case, literature, that is at issue. So a few more words on the ULA. Wenclas targets a number of people on his blog: the aforementioned Eggers, for example, Paul Auster and Rick Moody being amongst his recent victims.

> I've read Moody's *Ice Storm* and found it solipsistic, uninteresting, and afflicted with detail disease[...]That he is a mediocre writer of course isn't as important to us as the fact of his influential position in the lit world.

Almost as soon as the ULA was founded they began laying into Moody. In 2000, for example, they announced that he had just accepted a $35,000 Guggenheim grant even though he is from the family that founded Moody's Investors Service and is therefore likely to have more than enough money to fund his creative projects as it is.

The ULA has exposed many other such cases of abuse of funding by the well-heeled. A result being that millionaire Jonathan Safron Foer returned the cash portion of his recent 'needs based' NEA grant. All that's needed now is for an actual needy writer to get one of those grants in the first place!

It is not all attack-attack-attack however. Apart from organising events and publishing zines, along with blogs, reviews and commentary on the publishing industry (see the weekly Monday Report), the ULA have also published a number of new novels.

Fat on the Vine by Carl Robinson is published by ULA Press, an imprint of Out Your Back Door.com, the one-stop-shop for all your cultural needs.

Here's what publisher and ULA-er Jeff Potter has to say about it:

> *FAT* is a truly far-out novel. Transgressive in every way. Yet, yet, yet it's sweet and redeemed somehow. How? Hard to imagine but it works!
>
> Other novels today are tame and fakey by comparison...
>
> *Fat on the Vine* appeals to readers who fancy themselves as underdogs. It's about drugs, self-hatred and obsession. It's written without social filter or shame. The novel is as beautiful as it is disturbing.

And here's the blurb from the back to give you an idea of the kind of thing what we are dealing with here:

> What would you do if your name was 'lil big sexy' and you were a twenty-eight-year-old virgin and the first girl you ever slept with informed you the next day that she was a 'Nixon-lesbian'? What would you do if you lived in your parents' basement and your genteel, Christian mother followed you around all day singing spirituals and telling you that you were 'demon-possessed'?

Potter also published the ULA's first novel *The Pornographic Flabbergasted Emus* by Fred Wright – billed as a 'rockn'roll novel from the world of zines' – giving it the following blurb:

> The *PFE* is a very funny novel about a garage rock band in a college town. It's told from the point of view of the band members who are all housemates. So it's a house novel, too. But unlike most rock and roll novels – which tell the story of a band rising to stardom – Emus is the story of a local band that never makes it big but rocks on anyway.

The author is a longtime garage rocker himself. Possibly because of this the book has an interesting layout. It's set up like a rock song. Each chapter title has an A-side/B-side and a lead-in...

As is the rule with ULA Press projects, the *PFE* is more realistic, fresher, bolder – and thus funnier – than somewhat related work by big publishers. It's also bawdier, rougher, as if a real person wrote it instead of a committee buffed by profs and backed up by lawyers. ULA Press offers vital lit again for a change.

Author Wred Fright denies he was raised in the wild by emus, but he has played guitar and sung in such bands as The Escaped Fetal Pigs, Anal Spikemobile, Rage Against Dabney Coleman, and Team Fright. He currently roams the former USA serving as the Ohio Bureau Chief of the Underground Literary Alliance. He studied zines for his PhD – the first person to do so! His website is wredfright.com.

When he does readings he usually plays some quality thrash rock, too. He puts on a show. He has a surprise heckler/maniac sidekick. It's rock'n'roll.

The Riot Lit Collective

Before rounding off this brief look at the new wave of angry literary groups who have been making the most of the internet, we should mention the US based Riot Lit Collective. Being 'across the other side of the pond' as they say, this lot are of a similar ilk to the Underground Literary Alliance and are sympathetic with the aims of the BritLit groups mentioned earlier in the chapter, such as The Offbeat Generation and The Brutalists. The Riot Lit Collective declare that:

> We are your voice
> You are ours
> This is our revolution

and contributors and associates include Brad Listi (whose book *Attention Deficit Disorder* was an *LA Times* bestseller), Jeremy Robert Johnson (called a 'dazzling writer' by Chuck Palahniuck author of *Fight Club*), Christopher Young (author of *Click,* about which *Dogmatika* litzine say: '…a compelling genre-bending piece of fiction with a great hook. Click embodies the grit-lit of the streets…'), Tony O'Neill (*The Guardian* call his latest novel '… the next underground classic'), as well as N. Frank Daniels and Joseph Suglia and Jolene Siana. Not forgetting Daniel Scott Buck whose book *The Greatest Show On Earth* – unlike those of other members, who seemed to garner much praise and a fair bit of press attention – suffered from a complete lack of reviews on its release perhaps due to it being a print-on-demand title. Buck was clearly disgruntled:

> Last summer I sent my novel to over fifty major and minor newspapers, and I did not get a single review. I used to share cigarettes with one of the book reviewers of the *Portland Tribune,* a newspaper located on the same block as my office. He informed me that it was unlikely that the book would get reviewed because it was a print-on-demand novel; and he was right about that.

On the RiotLit MySpace site it seems to be Brad Listi, blogging from LA, who does most of the posting (perhaps with his bestseller credentials he has more money than the others and can afford the time?), and he is by no means afraid to stray from the remit of book blogging. See 'If Jesus was the King of MySpace, I wonder if he would have 147,031,267 friends?' or the run-down on his friend giving birth on the living room floor, photographs included (and censored!).

But Scott Buck also clearly enjoys delving into the world of book bloggers. Though aware of Bookninja, Blogspot.inc and Maud Newton, all online reviewers to whom he sent his book, it was Grumpy Old Bookman and Girl On Demand that finally took up the gauntlet to post reviews of his title – a good year and a half after it was published. But for a sample of Buck's lightly-humourous writing that does not relate to his own work here's what he has to say about the recent controversy generated by American author James Frey. Frey's memoir *A Million Little Pieces* has been faced with more than a few accusations of straying too far from the truth:

The Man Who Conned Oprah

...one reviewer after another seems to take an increasing amount of pleasure in developing a special vocabulary about the man ('Frey-watch'; 'Frey'em'). And I can't read or hear the name James Frey without thinking of Jennifer Lauck, and I cannot think of Jennifer Lauck without thinking about the concept of Subjective Truth and how, apparently, that is Okay by Oprah.

So I'm in the East Village for the weekend, visiting from Portland, Oregon. Sitting at the Pick Me Up Cafe, I'm talking to my wife on the cell. I'm here at this cafe for the wi-fi and the coffee, looking at a website on my laptop where there is a group photo from the RiotLit Reading at the KGB Bar the night before; and James Frey is in the photo.

I didn't know that I had actually met the man. I called my wife and asked her what she thought about the controversy.

'Oprah is the most powerful force in the publishing industry,' Mrs Buck says.

'So, I guess James Frey screwed up,' Mr Buck says. 'He got busted for pulling the wool over Oprah.'

'Well,' Mrs Buck says. 'Nobody fucks with Oprah.'

So I do a little research and find this posting about the James Frey controversy, posted by Jennifer Lauck herself on her own personal blog:

I think Mr. Frey should be thanking her. Look how many books he sold, in the beginning and now will sell and how much personal growth (which is priceless) he will receive from her efforts... Most of all, the entire US publishing

> industry should be thanking her.

But that's not all. Jennifer Lauck has some last words:

> We are all indebted to Oprah Winfrey and this is a debt that I am very intimate with. This is what I think about the James Frey controversy. Thank you, Oprah, for your committment to truth and thank you for all you do!

Truth? Truth? Truth? Jennifer Lauck has already told us her truth. Her truth happens to be historically incorrect. So I call my wife with this nugget.

'Here's further evidence of the failure of post-modernism,' Mr Buck says. 'If Jennifer Lauck praises Oprah for her commitment to the truth; this being, of course, after Oprah Winfrey's standing ovation for Jennifer Lauck's knack for telling lies, then how could you expect James Frey to amount to anything else? At least he tried to sell his book as a novel.'

'Ah, honey,' Mrs. Buck says. "Doncha see? Oprah Winfrey is the Architect of post-modernism for the 21st century. James Frey didn't pull the wool over her eyes. She pulled the wool over his!

I also enjoyed his post about working in a book shop as a student, when the book *American Psycho* was a dirty thing to be seen buying:

> I worked at a bookstore during these early years in college. It was a small room set in the back of a JK Gill's department store. There was an open entrance, slightly larger than your average door, for customers to pass through. The Book Section, as we called it, was lined with books on all four walls. I worked with an older woman, Barbara, who was quite shy but also very funny at times. She worked full-time back there, whereas I worked part-time because I was going to school. And it was easy work. The only hard part

was getting there on time. The arrival, as usual.

One day, a customer came in and asked for a particular book. I had never heard of the book before, and it wasn't on the shelf, so I offered to put in a special order (assuming the book existed, of course). And as I started to go through the paperwork, Barbara whispered, 'It's in the cabinet.' What she was telling me was that the book was in stock, just not on the walls. She unlocked a cabinet and pulled it out.

The book was *American Psycho* by Bret Easton Ellis. The look on Barbara's face, a severe frown, was all it took for me to want to read it. As I found out later, the controversy over *American Psycho* started before the book was published. The original publisher had dumped it, and it was picked up by an editor by the name of Gary Fisketjon at Vintage Contemporaries, and then released in paperback. Even if that meant it had to be sold behind closed doors in bookshops like the one mentioned above. It was a dark and hard-hitting book. It was The Cook, the Thief all over again. But with words…

The reality is this: The publishing world needs another Gary Fisketjon.

In the 80s and early 90s, Gary Fisketjon made a mark on the publishing world by publishing books that had a cutting-edge to them, even while the market was becoming saturated and ruined by Celebrity Bios and Trauma Memos. He has since gone on to work with some of the greatest writers in the world. And who could blame him? The man can't do everything.

What we need now is a Gary Fisketjon for our generation.

The LitBlog Co-op: remoulding tradition?

With recommended reads for new titles Spring 2007 including books that have yet to 'break through', like Alan De Niro's *Skinny Dipping in the Vale of the Dead* and *Wizard of the Crow* by Ngugi wa Thing'o, you might think that the US based Litblog Co-op is another example of freethinking litbloggers and writers who are keen to create a different mode of publishing, breaking free of the commission-publicise-publish-sell agenda dictated by most houses.

Not necessarily. The LitBlog Co-op has a members list which includes well-respected book bloggers whose names are quickly becoming familiar – such as Book Dwarf, Return of the Reluctant, Rakes Progress and Shaken Not Stirred – alongside slightly less familiar names – Slushpile, Literary Kicks and Pinky's Paperhouse for example. However, not everyone is keen to join. The collective has been criticised for operating in much the same way the mainstream publishers do, through their key 'Read This!' campaign, whereby five of the bloggers will each nominate a title they think is worthy of readers' attention, then the co-op will vote for one to promote jointly.

In brief, The LitBlog Co-op stand accused of trying to creating a 'big fuss' around a title through viral marketing before it comes out – a tactic which some bloggers find offensive.

Bookslut, for example, declined to join the Litblog Co-op or Virtual Book Tours, but she does agree to feature ads on her site, many for small press titles. (Apparently she briefly panicked when she realised she wanted to review a book that has an ad on her site, but went ahead anyhow. 'If people think I'm going to hawk a book in return for a $90 ad, they should probably read another blog! I'm glad we waited to take ads until now, though, because at first we were so thrilled that someone sent us a free book that our choices were dictated by that.' (From *The Village Voice 2005.)*

Maud Newton is another blogger who refuses to join not only because she is already too busy with her blog, a novel in progress, freelance book reviewing and her day job, She also objects to the Co-op's promotional strategies, preferring a more natural transference of ideas, through word of mouth and independent of publishing dates and industry agendas (*The Village Voice* as above). As she explains the situation:

> The Co-op does something like what the media do – it creates a big push for a book. If their goal is to prove the influence of blogs to publishers, I think they'll succeed – but it's not a goal I share myself.

Tactics aside, its goals are nonetheless admirable:

> Uniting the leading literary weblogs for the purpose of drawing attention to the best of contemporary fiction authors and presses that are struggling to by noticed in a flooded marketplace.

Besides, as the whole point of the enterprise was to see what a group of writers and bloggers could achieve in terms of pushing a title, the group can hardly be criticised for going all-out to do just that. As Mark Sarvas of the Elegant Variation, who is behind the LitBlog Co-Op, writes:

> We want to shine a light on literary fiction likely to get overlooked and lost in the shuffle... The mission is to see what happens when ten to twenty lit bloggers get behind a title and push hard. Does it make a difference?... We're casting a wide net to get a more eclectic view. We want to avoid the Philip Roths and Cynthia Ozicks, people who don't need help finding readers.' (*LA Times* 2005)

At the very least it is hoped that the effort will unify many of the discussions that had been hitherto fragmented among participating blogs. But perhaps it will achieve more besides perhaps the Litblog Co-op will actually make a difference in terms of sales figures and broaden the readership of the books that it supports.

Rebecca Gillieron

Review Pages vs. The Internet

Blogs: a parasite?

> The best blogs are wonderful tools and welcome simplifying resources. The worst of them are mini-altars of self-worship, which are obsessed mostly with how many 'hits' and how much 'traffic' they get than with the quality of their offering. How can you claim that a newspaper's 'wider readership' is a fallacy when one could just as easily allege that the number of pings and pongs and 'hits' a blog gets can be fixed by strategically linking to the most googled topics and names of the moment and to the sites of all of your blogger buddies?
>
> Shannon Byrne, Little, Brown

The activity of blogging about books has caused a surprising amount of friction within the publishing industry and related media circles. Book blogging was never going to be a wholly welcome addition to the world of book reviewing from the point of view of those who provide the mainstay of lit-crit in the national newspapers and magazines, but few could have predicted the hostility and wholeheartedly negative response that certain individuals have been voicing in recent months. Which, considering the types of criticism that is being raised, may be rather surprising. When, for example, the central objection from 'established' literary critics is that there is no quality control amongst book bloggers, and 'just anyone' can write and post reviews, it is a wonder they feel threatened at all by such worthless missives. Equally, when other criticisms focus on points such as the lack of internet traffic that book bloggers generate, it seems odd that literary critics of the major reviews pages even care about such trifles as book blogs – we might ask why industry figures bother commenting at all. But the fact is that print journalists are concerned. Perhaps the more interesting question should be, do they have any reason to be?

'Your mom's book club'

In the US there is an organisation called the National Book Critic's Circle (see Critical Mass, the blog) who in May 2007 picketed the Atlanta Journal-Constitution protesting against the fact that its book reviews editor Teresa Weaver had been sacked. All hell broke loose between book reviewers and book bloggers, with the *LA Times* quoting the book bloggers' attack on the critics:

> It's okay for the lit blogosphere to exist as a version of your mom's book club[...]it's okay for us to talk books and authors and compare notes on favorites, as long as we keep our place,' snapped the San Francisco writer, who runs the Return of the Reluctant website. 'We must not think for a minute that we contribute anything beyond serving as accessories to the real literary discussions.... We should buy books but not dare to offer well-thought opinions on them. (Attributed to lit blogger Edward Champion of Return of the Reluctant.)

Many of the so-called radical book bloggers are party to this view that they are ignored, that they are sidelined, using declarations of a so-called 'war' against the mainstream publishers as a *raison d'etre.* But are things really so bad for these book bloggers? Or are half of these people just indulging in some kind of pseudo-adolescent rant? When Edward Champion, for example, contributes reviews to the *LA Times* as well as running his website Return of the Reluctant, can't we imagine a healthy relationship of co-operation existing between the two spheres? Opinion is divided.

US blogger Maud Newton, who runs one of the more respected literary sites (maudnewton.com) is amongst those who remain puzzled by the idea that the two 'sides' are somehow competing. 'When bloggers disagree with or agree with an article about books in the mainstream press, it drives traffic to the newspaper,' she said. 'The cutbacks at newspaper book reviews are unfortunate, but hardly the fault of bloggers.' LA based blogger Mark Sarvas (of the aformentioned LitBlog Co-op and The Elegant Variation) agrees that the friction between reviewers and bloggers should be underplayed. 'This was truly a false dichotomy,' he claims, 'The two sides needn't be in opposition, certainly not at this time. There is a vast ecosystem of information about books out there, and all of it needs our support.'

Others are less forgiving. It is amusing to hear about the American 'Mistress' of online book group-bloggers at www.bookblog.net for example, who calls for the head of Little Brown's Atlanta-based publicist Shannon Byrne following her less than complimentary post on the 'parasitical' nature of book blogs. In the passage included here this 'Mistress' writes about her experience of meeting up with bloggers from the site in a local bar one night (it should be pointed out that not all book bloggers are anti-social nerdy types who lack the real life skills to communicate off-line and 'shock-horror!' in person).

> Eddie and I had stepped into the middle of a conversation between Levi and Miriam Parker, who surprised me when she said she worked at Little, Brown. Had I been in her shoes, standing among a lot of litbloggers, I might have said that I worked for Hatchette (the parent company) and saved Little, Brown for conversation with dead tree media. Miriam, though, was lovely... She graciously said I should let her know if there was anything from Little, Brown that

> I wanted, so, in my usual tact-filterless style, I asked for Shannon Byrne's head on a plate. Poor Miriam.

So what exactly was it that the now-infamous – in this circle of book bloggers anyhow – Shannon Byrne of Little, Brown had written, which might have caused such offense? Her article entitled 'Frankly My Dear, You Should Give a Damn!' posted on Thursday 17th May on www.bookcriticscircle.blogspot.com was basically geared towards a rejection of bloggers' war cries that print media is dead, that newspapers and their reviews pages are on the way out. Clearly incensed by such comments, her reactionary and impassioned post include retorts such as:

> Seems to me, then, that the majority of bloggers (not all of them) actually function to critique, organise, and sort actual media rather than to generate much original literary criticism or innovative content themselves.

She considered it outrageous that book bloggers were criticising the very sources of their information, and went on to claim that:

> ...blogs are kind of like parasitic microorganisms which feed off of a primary host. For the sake of this discussion, the host is clearly print media. Some are the good bacteria and some are transient and viral. Or maybe I can upgrade blogs to the status of some sort of interstitial or synovial fluid, buffering the vital organs of the media (newspaper, television, radio, the internet)? But, c'mon, if newspapers are dying, then blogs are the maggots come to feast upon their corpses...

The irony of the situation – with her complaining about the futility of blogs, in a blog – did not escape those readers that paid attention to her article. Blogger 'Jeff', for example, responds on the site, in some amusement:

> Ah, so now we're maggots. Gloating maggots. Lovely. Let's try this, how 'bout it, Shannon. Try to get your protest out there and try to generate interest in your campaign and make all of your complaints about blogs and their gloating ways without doing so ON A BLOG! Let's get ya to a Kinkos so you can run off a couple a thousand letters and then to the post office where you can take advantage of the perma-41 cent stamp to send it off to the world. Or maybe try and run your essay and an accompanying petition in one of the newspapers that still has book coverage. Or maybe sit outside a Krogers on a Sunday next to the guy giving out a free copy of the paper and a t-shirt if you'll subscribe. Hmm, doesn't work so well, does it?

Another reader, Dan Wicket can't help but poke fun at her a little, adding some statistics on the decline in newspaper sales, just to stoke the fire of debate a little:

> More reasons not to dash off posts while you're still very upset (that is, besides calling a respected author and editor a can of stew): The misguided 'dream' that newspapers are dying. This link is to a study by journalism.org using what appears to be reputable data. Over the course of the 1990s circulation in this country dropped 11%. The average newspaper bought per household was nearly 1 1/4 papers at one point and has dropped to barely over 1/2 a paper. If newspapers are not dying, they must at least be considered to be sick...

And when The National Book Critics Circle has itself launched a 'Campaign to Save Book Reviewing' that features (of all things!) a BLOG series, including posts by concerned writers, op-eds, Q-and-As, and tips about how you can get involved to make sure those same owners and editors know that book sections and book culture matter – well doesn't it all sound a little confusing?

Are these 'stalwart industry figures' sure they want to fight the bloggers? Are the bloggers sure they want to place themselves in opposition to reviews? It seems many are happy to throw out provoking comments into the arena with people like Pulitzer Prize-winning book critic Michael Dirda posting derogatory remarks like:

> If you were an author, would you want your book reviewed in the *Washington Post* and the *New York Review of Books*, or on a website written by someone who uses the moniker NovelGobbler or Biogafriend? The book review section…remains the forum where new titles are taken seriously as works of art and argument, and not merely as opportunities for shallow grandstanding and overblown ranting.

But there are no clear boundaries to the two alleged 'sides' and the continuing harping becomes wearisome. In the *LA Times* (May 2007) Josh Getlin refers to this fact that 'There is a growing sense that enough is enough – and that the friction between old and new book media obscures the fact that the two are in bed together now, for better or worse.' And he certainly has a point there.

Please! No more heads on plates.

It is useful, perhaps, to return to blogger Mark Sarvas of The Elegant Variation for his level-headed input on the matter. Rather than getting drawn too closely into this drawn out campaign to reinstate Teresa Waver at the Atlanta Journal Constitution (whom is claimed by the online petition to have looked-after 'one of the best-edited books pages in the country' www.petitiononline.com), he encourages us all to rid ourselves of hysteria and look at the broader picture. He is concerned about the trend for cuts in book reviews pages, but not because of any misplaced sentimentality for print media or refusal to embrace new forms of information exchange. Instead he wants to look to the future and consider 'How do people get their information today?', as this is the pivotal question around which all other concerns rotate.

In a two-part post featured on Critical Mass (the blog of the National Book Critic's Circle board of directors) he writes:

> I am divided, pulled in three directions – as a blogger, as a book reviewer, and as a novelist with a debut on the way. The blogger in me wants to say, above all, that[...]bloggers and print journalists are not – and should not be placed – in opposition. The story, as I keep suggesting, is much bigger than that.
>
> As a soon-to-be-published novelist, I can't help but watch with alarm as book review pages are hacked away.

There are a few things that we need to keep in mind, according to Sarvas, in order to get an objective grasp of the debate.

> ~ Beware the alarmists who are saying books will be killed by the internet... 'I side with those who take heart in the number of titles published each year, in the crowds in book stores and at events like the Los Angeles Times Festival of Books and PEN World Voices and who think it will take more than the disappearance of book pages from newspapers to kill books. They are made of sterner stuff.'
>
> ~ Beware the echo chamber: It's gratifying, indeed, to see so many writers come out in support of all this – or is it? I am struck that the proliferation of editors, reviewers and authors signing the petition all have a vested, financial interest in continuing book review pages...
>
> ~ The reader has the power: The readers have to respond, make their voices heard and – above all – their purchasing power felt... one certainly never sees the sports sections being cut...'

As he sees it, even if localised battles (in this case to save the *Atlanta Journal*'s books reviews pages) are won, there will be many more. Rather than celebrate the demise of reviews pages, book bloggers, publishers, readers and journalists alike, must pool their resources and work together to preserve this invaluable medium. For book reviews pages are not read simply for pleasure, they do not serve only to sway the purchasing power of the reader towards a particular author or trend. They are – in an ideal world at least – essential tools of cultural dialogue which stimulate informed debate, encourage new writing and shape the literary world.

Or are they? Well, the question is irrelevant according to Savas, who seems to require that we re-examine the role of the reviews pages in accordance with 21st century developments within the publishing industry. (And who is this Savas, that we should pay attention to him? Well, his credentials are good: The Elegant Variation was included amongst the *Guardian*'s 'Top 10 Literary Blogs' in 2006, it was one of *Forbes'* 'Best of the Week' and *Los Angeles Magazine* gave it the accolade of 'Top Los Angeles Blog' along with the comment: 'Really brave...or really stupid.')

> As much as I might agree in my heart with the notions of a newspaper's cultural obligations and the idea of reading as an ennobling act… I think it's a losing tactic in a fight, and I like to win. As newspapers are consolidated into the arms of mega-corporations, the only consideration is bottom line. And if readers don't make newspapers feel a financial impact of their choices they will only have themselves to blame.

He goes on to discuss publisher's role, laying some of the responsibility with them also:

> Similarly, publishers will need to start supporting book sections

> though advertising revenue. This notion that there's some entitlement to book coverage isn't a real world model. Scale back some of those money-losing advances, open up the pocketbook and place some ads in newspapers. Even if you don't the ad will sell books, it will help preserves your books pages – which will, in turn, sell books.'

He has a point. In the earlier part of 2007 in the US the *Los Angeles Times* cut the size of its book review section and redesigned it to share space with the 'opinion' section, book reviews pages were also cut in San Francisco and the *Chicago Tribune* moved its reviews pages to the Saturday paper, which has a smaller circulation. In all of these cases, publishers cited a lack of ad revenue generated by book reviews.

Of course some might not care. Savas points out that 'not all books reviews are created equal' or are good even, 'though there seems to be some unspoken assumption that they are, in fact some are dull.' Moreover – and this is a fact which from a publishers' point of view becomes infuriating – '...every newspaper covers the same dozen titles...' Of course if it's your own title that is riding the crest of the wave, picked up by the *Independent* only to have the *Guardian, The Sunday Times* and the *Telegraph* follow suit, then hey-ho who's complaining! But when you are trying to secure column inches for a new author who can't hope to get a look in amongst the three thousand ways of praising Zadie-Smith's-second-novel's-third-sentence's-final-nuance and so forth then the going can be tough indeed.

This lack of balance and variety in terms of the titles that reviewers are willing to cover is something that bloggers aim to redress. Like many other bloggers, Callie Miller, an LA-based blogger who runs Counterbalance, is aware that their medium enables readers to identify worthy authors – including local writers perhaps – who are ignored by the usual print media outlets. 'On any given Sunday, we see the same books reviewed in many publications, and then you see another similar block of books the next week,' Miller said.

'My goal is to go beyond that.'

And some online reviewers manage to achieve their aims, at the same time gathering more readers than they ever dared hope. Reviews pages featured on the blog Salon.com offer one such success story. Book critic Laura Miller writes reviews for the site that can gain up to four million viewers in a week. For more on this see Josh Getlin's piece on 'Books and Ideas', May 2007, from which the following quote was extracted:

> In a weird way, we're part of the establishment now,' Miller said, describing Salon's growth since its creation in 1995. 'And it sounds harsh, but you get what you pay for. We hired good writers. I used to write for peanuts, and you can't make a living doing that. So it may be that the friction between bloggers and reviewers is just another version of this age-old resentment that aspiring journalists have always felt toward more established journalists.

Perhaps the 'critics vs book bloggers' dispute creates not so much of a battleground, then, but more a playground fight amongst the pettier reviews and bloggers, who fail to see that coexistence is to the advantage of all, and that the greater aim – that of promoting good writing and encouraging and celebrating a genuine love of books – is what has driven this movement of book bloggers in the first place and continues to be the motivating force.

> 'I think cutting newspaper book coverage is an abject and unfortunate development,' said Champion in an email to *The Times*. 'I also think it's egregious for either of the two sides to wag schoolmarmish fingers at each other. The litblogs could use more editorial care; the newspapers could use more passion and spontaneity. But here's the good news: the twain can meet.'

Rebecca Gillieron

The Complete Review

One of the places which reviews Marion Boyars books is the Complete Review. When we receive a review from this website, it makes us lift our heads from whichever manuscript or computer programme we are currently cajoling into producing a finished book. The Complete Review, or Literary Saloon which it also calls itself, is an online review site which takes a great interest in translated fiction, and so we have had quite a few reviews in the past. It is also a good source of information about different countries and their writers, and contains useful links. This how the Complete Review describes itself:

> The Literary Saloon is the literary weblog at the complete review. It offers opinionated commentary on literary matters, as well as news from and about the complete review, literary news, links, musings, and the occasional tirade.
>
> Primary responsibility for the content on the site thus falls on ringleaders MAOrthofer and Elizabeth Morier, though diverse and sundry associates and acolytes provide valuable support and often also have their say.

The reason I have a wry smile on my face when a review from the Complete Review arrives in this office, is that they are the only review outlet which sends us publishers, and the authors of course, straight back to the school room. If the Complete Review is in a good mood with us, we get a B+. If, however, for some reason, we have not done our homework, we receive a B-. The only good thing about this is that books published by Penguin, with vast advances and publicity budgets, for example Merisha Pessl's *Special Topics in Calamity Physics*, gain a staggering a B-. However, *The Singing Detective* by Dennis Potter, gets an A, although this is a TV play available on DVD. Martin Amis gets a clutch of B-'s, except for his *The War Against Cliché* which gets an A–. Peter Carey also gets a whole lot of B's. I wonder if authors look at their results on the author listings on the site – it makes for fascinating reading but I do not think it is exactly encouraging, even to Booker Prize winners. Maybe their aim is to instill in people the fact that it is very hard indeed to become an accomplished and world renowned writer. If this is their aim, then do it very well indeed for I would not dare challenge any of their reviews or judgments.

Catheryn Kilgarriff

Book Blogs and Writers

The profession that must spend as great a percentage of their working life on the internet as any must be that of the writer. Of course, writers have historically worked in cold, draughty rooms or libraries, on their own, with little to look forward to in the afternoon for diversion other than doing what they did in the morning, naturally enough, which is to look out of the window.

This has all changed with the advent of the computer, with its wonderful link straight into other people's worlds. Many writers force themselves to write longhand with their computers turned off, to avoid the seductive 'ping' of the incoming email. I would think this would be too hard to do, since the whole point of the internet is that you are instantly connected with other people. I do agree that email should not be obsessively checked and what looks like a small crisis one day can be seen as a slightly time wasting diversion the next as the significance has paled away.

Authors are increasingly constructing their own websites and these can be a great source of erudite information. In a way, it is free writing and entertainment. But on some level, the website of a writer is also a promotional tool for their books. I am amazed that so few writers use this medium since it is almost free to use, and requires only the odd bit of effort on the writer's part.

Toby Litt's website has esoteric subject headings and I am pleased to show how very useful the internet is to him as he researches his novels. Litt is a writer who manages to combine the serious content in his novels with humour and is one of the most interesting writers around at the moment. His queries show the breadth of his curiosity, and of course, his need to connect with other individuals as he stays on the lonely path of the writer.

To be honest, there is probably not a huge amount of difference between the life of a contemporary novelist and that of a publisher in a small house. We work in environments which are more similar to a front room that an office, with more bookshelves than photocopiers and a total absence of tills and neon signs (how we expect to make a living given these surroundings is a mystery). We have more or less control over noise levels in the office and the company we keep, and we even get invited to the same parties and literary festivals. I read a small comment on Readysteadybook by Mark Thwaite recently, where he was bemoaning the fact that publishers put too little effort into their websites. His argument was that publishers are in a unique position to enthuse people with the contents of the books they publish. While I am often amazed at the small amount of information on the conglomerate's websites, especially when you consider how large their sales are, I do know that it's quite hard to distill into words the reasons why a particular author is felt to be worthy of publishing and marketing without degenerating into hyperbole and marketing-ese rather than language. So when an author is able to put in many words an approach to life which is also found in his novels, it's worth devoting some space to it in this book.

The section below from Toby Litt's website, www.tobylitt.com, is called 'Askings', where he hopes people who stumble across his site can help him with queries.

ASKINGS

If you know any of the answers, please email me.

NB Although some Questions are listed as having Answers, these are not necessarily definitive and I am always looking to learn more.

HIGH PRIORITY QUESTIONS

Does anyone know the full etymological meaning of any of these names?

Surnames:

Masaryk (Czech), Calixte (Haitian), Delira (Haitian), Auxilaire (Haitian), Myrthil (Haitian), Lu (Chinese), Akliku (Ethiopian), Sani Sokoto (Nigerian), Failte, Mposo, Lee, Quickborn, Zone, Bolland, Pandit, Ooki (Japanese), Aoki (Japanese).

First names:

Iqbal, Luckson, Ludger, Othniel, Cyril, Apara (Nigerian), Lij (Ethiopian), Ai (Japanese), Io (Japanese).

Does anyone know names in African or Indian languagues which have the following meanings:

Smith, Walker, Villager, House, Wood, Forest, Road, River, Waters, Stream.

Question from Simon Withers:

Incidentally I came across your site again just now while using Google to try to answer a question of my own: What is LITT5? I was browsing a pub review website looking the various locals near my new office and trying to find a congenial pub to meet somebody for a drink when I came across the following: http://www.beerintheevening.com/pubs/s/14/14576/Queen_Anne/Vauxhall 'Cracking pub with strippers. LITT5 & 3 are known to frequent on a Friday lunch/afternoon.' Now who/what the hell is LITT5? I searched on Google for LITT5 which threw up an interesting set of results, but didn't answer the question. So I searched for LITT, thinking that LITTs 5 and 3 are surely part of a larger family, and that's when I got back to your own website. Any ideas?

Did dinosaurs get cancer? (Feb 06)

In Albrecht Durer's engraving, 'Saint Jerome in his Study', 1514, why does St Jerome, writing right-handedly, have his ink pot on the left side of his desk? (Sep 05)

Is there a good online site to give you the meaning of African surnames? All the ones I can find are crap or cost money. (Sep 05)

Is there a branch of botany which deals with the area fifty to one hundred feet off the ground? Airborne botany? Aviated botany? What is it called? (Aug 05)

(After reading *Parallel Worlds* by Michio Kaku) If white holes exist, they must be spilling out some form of matter. And have been spilling it out for a very long time. We can't detect either white holes or dark matter (or dark energy). Perhaps dark matter comes out of white holes – and we could call it white matter. (June 05)

How big is the biggest family (number of children) in the UK? Not with adopted or stepchildren. All with the same mother and father. I'm guessing around fourteen. Anyone know exactly? (Dec 04)

Is there a name for those similes which wouldn't necessarily work, not unless one of the things being compared happened to have a quality it doesn't always have, that being the quality it is being used for? Example being, 'Hungry like the wolf'. Which really means 'Hungry like the wolf when the wolf is hungry'. This rather than 'Tall like a skyscraper'. Because a skyscraper has to be tall to be a skyscraper but a wolf doesn't necessarily have to be hungry. (Elvis knew about this. 'Her lips are like a volcano that's hot' – i.e. not a volcano that's extinct, which is just as much a volcano.) (Dec 04)

There's a quote from Norman Mailer I sometimes use in creative writing classes. It goes, 'When two men say hello in the street, one of them loses.' But I can't track it down. Help. (26 Oct 04)

Kafka wrote a couple of famous parables about China. But how did he know anything about the place? Had he read any books on the subject? Which books were available? Or was he just going on general knowledge? (5 Feb 03) Plus, are there any other mentions of China in either his letters or his diaries? (27 Nov 03)

BOB DYLAN QUESTIONS

At the very end of *Eat the Document,* Bob Dylan is seen singing a very lovely song, accompanied by Robbie Robertson, in a hotel room. What is it? Where can I get hold of it? (2 Aug 04)

In reference to Bob Dylan's song 'Serve Somebody' – a) has anyone ever called Bob 'RJ' or 'Ray'? b) why? (except for the sake of a cheap rhyme). (13 Jul 04)

In reference to Bob Dylan's song 'God On Our Side', did Judas Escariot have God on his side (seeing how the crucifixion and therefore the redemption of the entire human race couldn't have taken place without his betrayal – and I know Dante shoves him halfway up Satan's arse)? (13 Jul 04) God on our side answer.

Why did the cover of John Wesley Harding change colour from buttermilk to light grey? (20 Jun 05)

UNANSWERED QUESTIONS

Ref. De La Soul: How many times did the Batmobile catch a flat? (22 Sep 03)

When Michel Foucault visited San Francisco did he ever take time out from the bathhouses to visit Alcatraz?

QUESTIONS WITH ANSWERS

(but please let me know anything else you know on the subject)

(* equals new and exciting)

*****If you come across any references in interviews by rock or pop stars to deterioration in their hearing, tinnitus, etc, I'd really like to hear about it.

*****Is burnt toast really carcinogenic? Enough to worry about? (Feb 06)

****How does the human ear make wax? (Aug 05)

***I saw a very interesting tomb in Warsaw old town. It was in the Basilica of St John the Baptist, just on the left hand side as you go in. It showed a knight being embraced by a mitred bishop, or perhaps the Pope. This is the first time I've seen two men embracing on a Christian tomb. There was a Latin inscription which I didn't have time to write down. I'd be really grateful if anyone has any information about this, or about other tomb statues of a similar sort. It was a very lovely thing. (Jun 05) Warsaw tomb.

**Why are the fish on the Great Barrier Reef mostly shaped the way they are, i.e. thin when seen from any angle but the side, and then oblongish? I realise it's evolution, but what environmental factors cause them to be like this? Is this a stupid question? (10 Sep 02)

*When flax is harvested to make linen, is it dead? Also, when cotton is harvested to make, er, cotton, is that dead? (Sep 05)

How are rice cakes made? How do you make rice go puffy like that? (Sep 05)

There is a greater number of a. human beings or b. trees in the United Kingdom? (This question is posed in Ben Moor's Edinburgh show *Coelacanth*.) (Aug 05)

You know those wooden boxes for putting wooden shapes in (cylinder, oblong box, star, etc), well, my son's has eight holes, and none of the wooden shapes fit through the wrong hole. Mathematically, what is the maximum number of holes possible? (Also the maxiumum given the shapes have a maximum of twelve edges, which the cross has.) This number surely can't be infinite, but how can it be calculated? (Aug 05)

Why does cheap, pulpy paperback paper go wavy and weird on airplane journeys? (20 Feb 03) Paperbacks answer.

What kind of mental map does a squirrel have of a tree? When it leaps from one branch to another, is it improvising with very fast reflexes or following a set route it has many times taken? (Jun 05)

Has anyone compiled a top ten list of the first words that babies (English-speaking) say? (Mar 05)

Do all airliners (or planes) have to have a curlicue spiral shape in their jet engines? And is it to show which way the turbines turn? (Jun 05)

Who designed the red and white Solidarnosc logo? Do they get royalties? (Jun 05)

Which film is it where the plot involves a group of passengers on a cruise liner on their way to heaven through a sea of clouds? I think it's 1940s or '50s and in black and white. (13 Jul 04)

Is there a good book or CD on how to identify British regional accents? (14 Sep 03)

What is a 'curmbox'? The word appears as my hotmail account is loading.

Where does that fluffy, scummy stuff come from that seems to end up in the bottom of a glass of water in which home-made ice cubes have melted? (Or maybe this is just London water.) A question which came up in China. Why or how is it that different cultures, from a long way back, have dragons as part of their folklore? Chinese dragons aren't all that dissimilar from Welsh. Do they have a common origin? (8 Dec 03)

When I was in China I saw a 'forthy-three storey ivory ball' – with forthy-three separate ivory balls recessed inside one another. What I want to know is, how exactly is this done? There was a diagram of three stages, but it wasn't particularly helpful. (27 Nov 03) When was the Cenotaph in Hong Kong built? Any interesting facts about it? (27 Nov 03)

I remember a television series from fifteen or twenty years ago with started with a series of long tracking shot, moving in towards the vanishing point. Each one was of a road or a field. Eventually (I think) a house or a door was reached. This was accompanied by lugubrious pseudo -classical music. It wasn't Heimat, was it? (13 Jul 04)

I read this in *The Age* newspaper, Melbourne, 'The two Koreas are technically still at war, and recently fought a battle in the Yellow Sea.' Do you know about this? Was it reported anywhere?

(10 Sept 02)

Why is nothing that we eat in England made out of pigs' milk? (14 Sep 03)

Has there ever been a heretical Christian sect that believed primarily in the Holy Ghost and not so much in the Father and the Son? (6 Jan 04)

Where in the world is 'Leeks Hills'? It's the title of one track on Brian Eno's Ambient #4: On Land. I can't find it anywhere in England.

Is whether there is an economic term to express the mutually beneficial relationship between supposedly unrelated manufacturing industries, such as sweet-makers and toothpaste-makers? (15 Sep 03)

During a discussion with writer Pauline Melville the question came up of who was a) the ugliest writer ever and b) the best looking. For a) she suggested George Eliot (harsh). For b) Byron (I disagree – sexy he may have been). Any better suggestions? (2 Oct 02)

'It is hard to think of an occasion in a novel of [Henry] James when a real taste is tasted or a real smell smelled.' So writes Seymour Chatman in *The Later Style of Henry James.* Anyone got any examples to contradict? (5 Feb 03)

Is gambling in any way subversive of capitalism? What is the most moving book you've ever read? (14 Aug 02) What is the most affecting film you have ever seen? (14 Aug 02) This isn't really an asking, but I'd like to start collecting the nicknames of crew on movies or TV. You know, the guys who are called something like Fred 'Bear' Dink in the credits. If you spot any good ones, let me know.

I'm interested in post-nuclear holocaust and other End of the World novels, comics, films and TV shows. Anyone got any good examples? (Jun 03)

What is the accepted Catholic doctrinal explanation of Jesus' words on the cross, 'My God! My God! Why hast thou forsaken me?' How is it possible for one part of the trinity to be divorced from the rest? (And please don't just say that's the true mystery of the incarnation.) (4 Nov 02)

Following the controversy over turnouts at the Countryside march and the Stop the War alliance march, do you know how the police really make their estimates of how many people turn up for a demo? (2 Oct 02)

How can I tell the difference between a swallow and a swift? (14 Aug 02)

What is the name of that clear stuff used to stick giveaway CDs to the covers of magazines? Who makes it? Is it a plastic or what?

Do you know the dates between which Penguin classics and Penguin modern classics were a certain colour? For instance, when did orange spines come in? (2 Oct 2)

I'm trying to put together a list of the lifemasks and deathmasks that have been taken from the faces of famous people (particularly writers). I've got a few so far (Keats, Cromwell, Swift) but if you come across any references, please let me know. Why not flush when the train is in the station? (4 Nov 02)

Is there a biological reason why a human being and one of the great apes of either sex can't have an ape-baby together? Aren't we 99.9% genetically similar? (20 Feb 03)

Whatever happened to David Band, who used to design record covers for Altered Images and Aztec Camera?

What is the word for the phenomenon of people having jobs that are related to their name, i.e. Mr Payne the anaesthetist, Mrs Proudfoot the chiropodist, and Mr Toby Litt the writer? (10 Sep 02)

What is the shortest English word containing all the vowels, 'a e i o u', in that order and also in any order? (14 Aug 02) So what choice diseases can one catch from a dodgy toilet seat? (ref: smallpox anxiety, recent viewing of *28 Days Later...*) (4 Nov 02)

I am interested in references to 'the North-West Passage'. What is the earliest that can be found? (18 Jan 03)

I'm interested in finding out about Bill Oddie's musical career. There was recently a letter from him in MOJO. If you have any information, I'd like to hear. Goodies' bootlegs?

Any suggestions for cult books I might write about?

I once read a book called, I think, Door into Dark. Until recently I remembered this as being by C.J.Cherryh, but I couldn't find it listed at the British Library. It was a fantasy novel, not by Seamus Heaney. Any ideas who it was by?

Back in the late 70s, a reporter from, I think, the BBC programme *Nationwide*, went 'under cover' with the homeless in London(?). I remember that he almost got beaten up, and had to be rescued by his film crew. Do you know anything more about this? Which reporter was it?

I think I know this one, but I might as well check. I recently took a flight in a British Airways plane (a Jetstream I think), which appeared to have both propellers and jets. It reversed out of its parking space, then went forwards – all without changing the direction of its propellors. Now, I'm assuming that it did this by altering the angle of the blades on the propellers. Am I right?

Which is the most 'environmentally friendly', hand towels or hand dryers? Also, if an escalator is running, does it save any energy/electricity to take the stairs instead?

Ever heard of a Scottish band called 'The French Impressionists'?

Does London, or failing that England, have any pachinko parlours? And if not, why not?

I recently saw a print, taken from a painting, called 'Dante and Beatrice'. It looked late pre-Raphaelite. Quite technically adept - good perspective, etc. Dante stands on the right of the picture, on a bridge, hand on heart, just having seen Beatrice, one of three, striding along. Who is it by?

What percentage of penalties are scored in the average English football season? Or, even better, what percentage of penalties have been scored since the beginning of the modern game? As the years pass, are more or less successfully converted?

Name any songs which use birdsong as backing, at any point, beginning, middle or end.

Can you list the name of every character Elvis played in every movie in which he appeared, in chronological order?

Do you, or do you know anyone, who would choose - of their own free will – Virgin Cola over either Coke or Pepsi?

Does anyone have a full chronological list of everyone who has turned on the Blackpool illuminations? And also the Regent Street lights. (No answer yet.)

Which is more disgusting: being stuck on a crowded, sweaty bus or a crowded, sweaty underground train? Reasons?

ANSWERS

From Ondrej Sefcik (6.06):

The surname 'Masaryk' is not in fact of Czech origin, but Slovak one, but it is very similar to common Czech surname 'Masaøík'. Both surnames are derived from Slovak *masar* and Czech dialectal (Moravian and Silesian) *masaø* 'butcher' (derived from *maso* 'meat'). Derivative suffix -yk or -ík has deminutive meaning, so *Masaryk* means in Slovak (but sounds so in Czech ears) 'little butcher'.

PS: There is a Czech word masaøka, Slovak masarka, which means 'Blowfly with iridescent blue body; makes a loud buzzing noise in flight'.

From M Knight (24.7.06)

Calixte may be related to Callistus, which is the Latinised form of the Greek *kallistos*, meaning 'most beautiful'.

Catheryn Kilgarriff

What makes a writer's blog good?

There are many writers whose daily musings would have made for fascinating reading. Imagine Louis Ferdinand Celine recounting tales from the hospital bedside with his acerbic wit and nose for adventure (don't hold back on the bile Louis!) or Colette letting us all in on her nocturnal indulgences. Or – let's go further afield – Nabakov chasing butterflies across the fields of his motherland (or in Central Park, NYC in latter years) I'd like to read about that... Virginia Woolf spitting furious rants against the long-suffering Leonard of an afternoon, wanting to break free from the suburbs 'If it is a choice between Richmond and death, I choose death!'

There's no denying that a little drama goes down well.

But what of writers of the here-and-now? Can the daily reflections of HarperCollins's or Random House's latest prodigy measure up to this brief fantasy of blogging writers? If the author's life is not so colourful as these large-than-life literary greats, can they nonetheless sustain a compelling narrative that charts the highs and lows of a wordsmith's daily existence? The short answer is that when 'joe blogs' is allowed to give blogging a go with no preconceived requirements to fill then so should our contemporary authors. So some people think that art and literature should not be judged with reference to the creator, and may argue that knowing the minutiae of a writer's daily existence may unduly affect our understanding of their work. But who cares? When reading the blog of aa favourite author is like being given the go-ahead to poke around in your friends' cupboards or snoop through someone's diary it's hard to resist. The question is, what makes a writer's blog good? You want personal info, you want a privileged vantage point granting direct insight into their minds and lives, but you also want to hear about their work, how they work, how their imagination operates, where their ideas come from, any problems they encounter in writing...and on top of that you want their views on others' work, their views on literature in general, their response to current affairs – the works! Enthusiasm in these situations is not necessarily exhaustive...

According to Colin Brush, Senior Copywriter at Penguin Books, in answer to the question 'What makes a good author's blog?' (June 2007) the writing:

- Should be personal – but not mundane
- The author should write about their work as well as their interests
- They should be entertaining company
- Posts should be regular and frequent

The writers' blogs he recommends include Neil Gaiman, author of *Fragile Things and American Gods* and many other novels, as well as the children's book *The Day I Swapped My Dad for a Goldfish*. Gaiman has been blogging since 2001 when his publisher set up the blog to promote *American Gods* and he now reaches over one million hits per month so he must be doing something right.

Here's some advice Gaiman offers from his blog to other writers: Firstly on the experience of being a writer, and then on how to go about getting published:

Tuesday February 3rd 2004

On Writing

I'm not sure what getting into a creative writing programme has to do with being a writer. Go and look at Teresa Nielsen Hayden's list of the fourteen things a slush-reader or editor is looking for and whether you've done a creative writing programme, have an MFA in writing, or are in fact currently teaching a course in creative writing isn't on the list.

(For the record, I've never been involved in a creative writing programme. In my case, that was mostly because I knew I wanted to be a writer, and had enough hubris to know that I'd rather make my mistakes on the job. It was also because I had a vague suspicion that people in authority might suggest that I should write respectable but dull fiction, and then I'd be forced to kill them, and it would all end in tears or in prison. Many of my friends have enjoyed creative writing programmes no end. Some of them teach them.)

As for giving up, well, sure, if you want to. Being a writer is a very peculiar sort of a job: it's always you vs a blank sheet of paper (or a blank screen) and quite often the blank piece of paper wins. It has no job security of any kind, and depends mostly on whether or not you can, like Scheherazade, tell the stories each night that'll keep you alive until tomorrow. There are undoubtedly hundreds of easier, less stressful, more straightforward jobs in the world. Personally, I can't think of anything else I'd rather do, but that's me.

If you want to be a writer, write. You may have to get a day job to keep body and soul together (I cheated, and got a writing job, or lots of them, to feed me and pay the rent). If you aren't going to be a writer, then go and be something else. It's not a god-given calling. There's nothing holy or magical about it. It's a craft that mostly involves a lot of work, most of it spent sitting making stuff up and writing it down, and trying to make what you have made up and written down somehow better.

I think for me the tipping point was when I was a very young man. It was late at night, and I was lying in bed, and I thought, as I often thought, 'I could be a writer. It's what I want to be. I think it's what I am.' And then I imagined myself in my eighties, possibly even on my deathbed, thinking that same thought, in a life when I'd never written anything. And I'd be an old man, with my life behind me, still telling myself I was really a writer -- and I would never know if I was kidding myself or not.

So I thought it might be better to go off and be a writer, even if what I learned from the experience was that I wasn't a writer. At least that way, I'd know.

Gaiman is aware that the internet is an essential tool in the quest for publication:

> If it's input you need, find a helpful bunch of like-minded people, either in real life or on the web. And, as mentioned here before, there's Clarion and Clarion West and Viable Paradise among others for the would-be SF-Fantasy writers. The SFWA has a list of workshops and groups, both virtual and visitable at www.sfwa.org/links/workshops.htm#yearly.

But he is understanding also of the requisite psychology that his profession demands: As he says, you have to be single-minded almost to the point of lunacy:

> It does help, to be a writer, to have the sort of crazed ego that doesn't allow for failure. The best reaction to a rejection slip is a sort of wild-eyed madness, an evil grin, and sitting yourself in front of the keyboard muttering 'Okay, you bastards. Try rejecting this!' and then writing something so unbelievably brilliant that all other writers will disembowel themselves with their pens upon reading it, because there's nothing left to write. Because the rejection slips will arrive. And, if the books are published, then you can pretty much guarantee that bad reviews will be as well. And you'll need to learn how to shrug and keep going. Or you stop, and get a real job.
>
> **How does one get published?**
> How do you do it? You do it. You write. You finish what you write.
>
> You look for publishers who publish 'that kind of thing', whatever it is. You send them what you've done (a letter asking if they'd like to see a whole manuscript or a few chapters and an outline will always be welcome. And stamped self-addressed envelopes help keep the wheels turning.) Sooner or later, if you don't give up and you have some measurable amount of ability or talent or luck, you get published. But for people who don't know

where to begin, let me offer a few suggestions: Meet editors. If you're into SF, Horror or Fantasy, go to the kinds of SF, horror or fantasy conventions that editors go to (mainly the big ones – look for words like WORLD or NATIONAL in the title). Same goes for romance or crime. Join associations – SFWA or HWA or the Romance Writers of America or The Society of Authors. Most organisations like that have an associate membership for people who wouldn't qualify for a full membership. Even if you haven't met any editors, send your stuff out.

The 'slush pile' of unsolicited manuscripts is not always a bad thing – publishers take enormous pleasure in finding authors from the slush pile (Iain Banks and Storm Constantine are both writers who simply sent out manuscripts to publishers), although it occurs rarely enough that it has to be a special thing when it happens. If you write short stories, don't worry about agents, just find places that might print the stories and get them out there. If you write novels, I think it's six of one, half a dozen of the other. I'd written and published three books before I decided it was time to get an agent.

Writers' groups can be good and they can be bad. Depends on the people in them, and what they're in them for. On the whole, anything that gets you writing and keeps you writing is a good thing. Anything that stops you writing is a bad thing. If you find your writers' group stopping you from writing, then drop it. The other thing I'd suggest is Use The Web. Use it for anything you can – writers groups, feedback, networking, finding out how things work, getting published. It exists: take advantage of it. Believe in yourself. Keep writing.

If only all writers were so dedicated, and so careful about who they approach regarding publication…

Jeff Vandermeer is another writer that gets a mention, who writes the blog formerly known as VanderWorld, now Ecstatic Days, from his home in Tallahasse. Award-winning author of fantasy novels including *Veniis Underground* (2003) *Shriek: An Afterword* (2006), he also contributes a comic book reviews column for Bookslut, writes SF reviews for the *Washington Post* and even gets the occasional review himself (this glowing analysis is from the *Washington Post* on *Shriek*):

> Like some delicious mash-up of HP Lovecraft, Mervyn Peake, and Frank Baum, but with his own verbal dexterity and perverse ingenuity…An affecting narrative about love, art, sibling rivalry, commerce, history, and some really nasty 'shrooms.'

Of his own writing, often labelled 'New Weird', and discussing fiction in general he writes that:

> Fiction isn't about naming but about avoiding being named. If a piece of fiction can be neatly and accurately labelled, then either the labeller is missing something or the fiction itself is in some way lacking. And yet we are obsessed with labelling, with naming. We label to sell fiction. We label to promote our own academic careers. We label because we want to stir up controversy. But all these labels obscure what is true about a great work of fiction: that it is organic, it is not one thing. It is a fish swimming through a reef, not a fish gutted on a dock.
>
> My style is intensely visual, but with the visual not a stand-in for characterisation or for plot. My style comes out of the sense that images have resonance, and that image can be a catalyst for action or character, but it's also flexible because each story requires some variation of a style to be effective. People have called my style 'baroque' or 'lush', but within this particular sub-spectrum of style there are many different ways to tell a story. And more of my recent fiction has had a more stripped-down style. So it's somewhere between Mervyn Peake and Martin Amis, probably. I'm not as stylised as Angela Carter, although I love her work.
>
> (From an interview on wotmania.com)

By all accounts Vandermeer's blog is no less appealing. Take the following comments on the craft of the wordsmith, posted alongside a photograph of five giant fish pens in bright colours, this is not a tortured missive from your average struggling artist:

> …knowing I'm going to be able to visit the Black Dog Cafe by Lake Ella every morning this week and just write longhand in my notebook with my fish pen (form-fitting to my hand and thus not an affectation) for as many hours I want, before coming home to spend the afternoon editing the New Weird anthology.
>
> Happiness is writing about people trying to cope with huge levitating bear creatures and intelligent sea anemones and rotting cities and swimming pools full of mushrooms and a giant grub and alcohol minnows and info beetles and love and death and everything in between.
>
> Almost nothing is better than just writing for me. And getting to that place where something clicks on and you're just a hand, writing, while the brain just watches.

No ego there then. More of a Jungian state of consciousness where the human is just the portal for these pre-existent ideas to seep through to the land of the living. I like it. And despite being a 'very busy man' (not his own words I hasten to add, I just notice he reviews for *The Washing Post* also) the man still finds time to ask for more – more books to be sent to him, more recommendations, more discussions:

> ***Washing Post* SF/F Round Up and What've You Been Reading? – July 21st 2007**
>
> *The Washington Post* has published my SF/F round-up reviews with the paper version appearing tomorrow.
>
> I'd say that *Brasyl* by McDonald, *Shelter* by Palwick, and *Bright of the Sky* by Kenyon are all books you should buy and read. All of

them will appeal to both brain and heart.

I agree with Cory Doctorow, who thinks Brasyl is McDonald's best yet. It is simply amazing, in my view.

Shelter is an ambitious, sprawling novel of the near future by Palwick that does a great job of extrapolation. Amazing characterisation, too.

Bright of the Sky by Kenyon is the start of a series that, despite a frame I didn't like as much, could well become a classic in the field.

And, even though I'm drowning in books right now, I'd like your suggestions. What've you been reading recently you really liked…or hated?

We have mentioned just a few writers here, but with the last two being male I am immediately aware of the need to redress the gender balance and include a female author in the pit of 'writers who blog' here. Remember *Oranges Are Not the Only Fruit?* You don't get more personal than Jeanette Winterson (who writes a column, which is updated monthly, on her website – see www.jeannettewinterson.com/column.asp):

Some days are like this – nothing really gets done and what does get done is pointless. Then, out comes a poem or a cat, or a flower, or a sunburst, or even a good piece of cheese, and the tilted world rights.

I admit it, I am struggling with my life at the moment – not my work life or my inner life, but the how to manage the incessant ignorant demands of senseless life. The bureaucratic nosy-parker form-filling time-wasting email-crazy, texting nightmare, junk sham of life that technology has locked us into. I seem to have spent all day today talking to Call Centres, arranging paperwork for VAT returns, filing receipts, checking out travel data, and it's the mental equivalent of stuffing your face with Big Macs.

The more real work I do the less tolerance I have for the unreal world called real life.

Maybe I should take up Yoga...

I am very tired after finishing *The Stone Gods*, my new book for adults. Where there are no limits, the first task is to discipline the self into focus. That done, there must be no self-consciousness about what happens next. The thing has to flow freely until the possibility of an edit, which happens in a different part of the brain. Poor writers are either too rigid – like a pre-formed pond liner, or too undisciplined, like a bog. The reader then sinks or hits the sides. The ideal is to allow flow, both for the reader and the writer, but this cannot be taught in a Creative Writing class, which is why they are utterly pointless, except from a sociological or psychological point of view – and maybe an economic point of view, unless you are the one paying.

I'm not being fair – you can turn out perfectly good jobbing writers via the Creative Writing class, but they are not writers I would ever want to read. Life is short – the obvious is, well, obvious; I don't need to find it in fiction.

I am feeling this way because I have been sent so many 'product' books recently. Identical fiction-robots all doing the same thing. Needless to say, they have all been on more programmes than your average alcoholic.

I suppose in a world of no job security and short contracts, finding a continuous narrative is important. Maybe that is why so many people want to write. There has to be some storyline, and the world of work no longer offers it, and perhaps it is not there in peoples' personal lives either.

I don't want to discourage anyone from writing, but unlike playing an instrument, people really can't tell if they are not very good at it. The thing about playing an instrument, however badly, is that it gives you insight into what it takes/means to play well. There is humility involved in the amateur pleasure. I get the most discordant rubbish sent to me, with no sense at all of how bad it is, or why. And people get very very cross if you decide to tell them why.

But never mind. The internet is democratising publishing. Put it out there and let the world decide.

I have a new cat called Spiky. The great thing is that he understands English, and I know that he is one of my Special Cats, which a writer like me needs, as a familiar, and as something to throw the paperweight at. Before you all have a fit, the paperweight is rubber, and the cat chases it.

Back to serious matters. I recently saw the opera *Death in Venice,* in a production by Deborah Warner. The production was wonderful but I struggled with the music. And then I saw it again, and still struggled. Then, listening to Radio 3 last Saturday night, as I always do if I am by myself, the opera slot was *Death in Venice,* so I heard it again. This time, it happened. The music made sense, intellectually and emotionally. I could hear it. It was wonderful.

This is worth thinking about. I go to the opera frequently and I am familiar with the shapes and the demands of the music. I am intelligent and I concentrate. Nevertheless, it took me three times to hear this music. Had I heard it twice I would probably not have found it at all in this life-time.

The point is that sometimes art in whatever form is effortful and we have to keep at it – or if we don't, we must be very careful not to just dismiss the piece. I would never be rude about Benjamin Britten's music, I love it, but I thought this opera was too fragmented. It isn't – something in me was too fragmented to hear the connections , and then, presumably my brain reconfigured and found the line.

It is a problem in a fast-food world, making time for the pace and rhythms of art. It is a problem finding our own pace and rhythm, and then being true to that, and then allowing it to flow with what we find elsewhere.

We're back where we started, and the rhythms of the inner and the outer. I think I was too jangled, too discordant, to hear the music. It is a difficult piece – my friend the cellist Natalie Clein tells me so, and she is top of the tree. Nevertheless, I failed to reach the music until the third time, and then the music reached me.

It was pouring with rain that night, and I found a landing place.

Perhaps that is all we need.

For a more alternative approach from a lesser-known wordsmith, try the blog from poet, performer and veteran of the London Underground Francesca Beard (though since giving birth to her daughter she has, understandably, been posting less frequently than the norm…) Born in Kuala Lumpur and having grown up in Penang, Malaysia, since moving to London Beard has toured the world with support from poetry group Apples and Snakes, and published her own collection of poetry which is in its fifth printing. Labelled variously 'Spine-tingling…witty and narcotic' by the *Independent,* 'The Queen of British Performance Poetry' by the *Metro* and 'Just as long as it makes you happy' (this last from her mother) Beard is equally happy to perform alongside well-established poets like Michael Rosen at larger venues like The Royal Festival Hall as at some grimy North London boozer.

Here's a few comments from her on appearances at festivals this year and last.

Chinese Whispers at KLP: 28th - 30th September 2006

Friday, October 20th 2006, 4:42pm

I did three shows of 'Chinese Whispers' at the gorgeous Kuala Lumpur Performing Arts Centre. Above is a picture of the park in which it sits. Across the way, there's a koi carp breeding farm and a Japanese tea house that serves dumplings and bowls of noodle soup – perfect pre-show food.

The second show was by far the best. In order to jazz up one of the interviews I was giving beforehand, Reezal and Sunitha from the British Council, arranged for 'Auntie', a highly skilled reflexology masseuse, to come to the dressing room and rub my feet, while I mused about where my ideas came from and what inspired me to write. The experience has ruined me – how can I now be expected to get on stage without an hour of being rubbed with oils?

Earlier that day, my dad, who was travelling with me in order to help look after Lola Choo, had looked at the schedule and exclaimed that my interviews were an hour and a half each - 'Julia Roberts only does two minutes!' he said.

I explained that Julia was a bit more famous than me and that this was the rate of exchange for a performance poet.

Now, I'm wondering whether Julia would still stick to the two minute rule, if she had 'Auntie' massage her feet during interviews.

***

A day or so after we got back from Malaysia, I was off to Cheltenham, to perform 'Chinese Whispers' in the Cabaret tent at the Literature Festival. Sarah Jane Arbury has been programming the spoken word events there for a while and I'd met her a few times here and there, but it was the first time I'd done Cheltenham.

It is quite grand in the Writers' Room. Intimidatingly forceful lady historians in stylish wool suits and sensible yet extravagant shoes crumble scones next to wine-swirling jet-set novelists. How comforting to see Patrick Neate eating a cheese sandwich in the corner. With nothing but his scowl, a stolen cheese sandwich and stories about how his laptop got stolen and the fact he's in massive sleep deficit, he managed to pep me up about pretty much everything. He's like the reverse of Pollyanna – somehow, the grumpier he gets, the more cheerful I end up feeling. He really is a lovely man. He's moving Book Slam to a new venue – perhaps you might like to find out more here: http://www.bookslam.com.

I also met writer Marcus Chown who, with his partner, randomly came to see Chinese Whispers. We got talking afterwards about quantum mechanics, as you do - see, I have a song about Shroedinger's Cat in the show. He's written some fabulously exciting books that I'm looking forward to reading - here's a picture of them – *The Universe Next Door* and *The Quantum Zoo* – geek heaven. Thank you Marcus, thank you Patrick and thank you Sarah Jane for inviting me and Chinese Whispers up – we had a great time.

But enough about poets. If you want to look at more writers who blog, along with those previously mentioned it is worth also looking at the blog of novelist, children's writer and playwright Susan Hill (recommended by Jeanette Winterson and found at www.susan-hill.com), or for a change from fiction writers try Noam Chomsky at www.chomsky.info.

In fact I will round off this section with a post from the blog of the former, Susan Hill, as judging from the type of posts she delivers she is apparently super-active within the blogosphere.

Writing almost daily on her website, the other blogs she recommends include Dovegreyreader, the Book Bar, Random Jottings of a Book Lover, Me and My Big Mouth, SnowBooks and Grumpy Old Bookman. However, it is this missive on the 'word of mouth' phenomena that catches my eye. It's great to hear such vehemence, determination and a fiery spirit. Susan Hill is a writer who is very much aware of how the industry works and fiercely protective of the role that book bloggers are carving for themselves within this industry. Not all writers operate from ivory towers, least of this woman.

The Holy Spirit Bloweth Where is Listeth.
Friday July 27th 2007

The wonderful Biblical phrase is applicable in many contexts and in this one, a bookish one. I am interpreting it as 'Word of mouth cannot be bought or done to order.'

Some years ago a good friend of mine came for coffee. As I was filling the kettle from the tap she asked if I didn't ever worry about what was in tap water. I said no. She said I should. She asked if I had ever thought of buying a water filter. No, I said. She said I should. Then she said, 'Well if you ever do, I can recommend someone who does sell them and they are very very good ones.' I knew her well. I looked her in the eye. 'Are you getting commission if I buy one from him ?' She had the grace to blush. Later, when she had given it up, having been sussed out too many times by her old friends, she said she had been on a course where they had taught her how to 'drop the subject of water filters casually into a conversation.' They didn't teach you very well, was my reply.

Now... we all know how it works. We have friends who read. We love a book. We tell them about it. On the blog. Off the blog. Some friends even ask us for suggestions. On or off the blog. Many of us regular book bloggers get new books sent by publishers and if we like them we say so. If not, we ignore them. No one pays us. No one influences us. It`s one of the best level playing-fields in the world. Ah but some clever bugger has discovered word of mouth and thinks it can be bought and influenced after all. Penguin has employed Buzz Marketing to generate 'anticipation' for a book through BzzAgents, who are 'ordinary people, encouraged to spread news about a title through book clubs, emails, blogs and online reviews, by – wait for this – CARRYING IT AROUND AND DISCUSSING IT AT PARTIES.

Now listen up Penguin, Buzzmarketing and anyone else thinking of trying this trick. We`ve got your number. If anyone tries a buzz on me they`ll get a buzz in the ear. I give my friends and my blog book recommendations UNINFLUENCED BY ANYONE. It will continue thus. If I went to a party, which I don`t, and someone came up to me all casually with a book under their arm, I'd tell them to buzz off.

Be assured that no book mentioned and praised and recommended by me on this blog or elsewhere has ever been done so as a result of any form of bribe or 'buzz.' If a publisher has sent it to me free, I say so. If I do not, you can assume I have either bought it or been given it by a friend. I know publishers want to sell books. I should. I`m a publisher. I will try to sell Long Barn Books in all sorts of ways. And I will give copies away in the hope that people will like it and recommend it. But that's the extent of it. Word of mouth between booklovers is a sacred thing and do you know why it works so well? Because we trust one another, that's why.

The Holy Spirit Bloweth where it Listeth.

Water filter anyone ?

Rebecca Gillieron

Book clubs with an online presence

I would like to join a book club, I sometimes think. Although I'd have to turn up with a brown paper bag over my head since I would prefer it if no one knew that I was a publisher. However, so far I have found that the only groups I know of near where I live have been going for years and are full or else they are at our local Waterstone's at 11.30am on a Thursday when I am busy working, so it hasn't happened.

The largest free book club in the world is one I have read about, but never actually noticed in practise – the bookcrossing network. The premise is simple. If you have had the experience of reading a book and wanting to tell another person about it, then simply take your copy off your shelf and leave it on a park bench or in a café, where it can be picked up by another person and enjoyed. I think you are encouraged to leave a note in the book making clear it is available, and now free, and perhaps saying why you liked it.

The bookcrossing premise is a good one and it is rather sweet – a bit like the scene in the Norwegian film *Elling,* where one of the characters goes repeatedly into a supermarket and inserts his poems in packets of food. It's literature as an unexpected gift, and can only be a good thing.

However, book clubs are also events where people interact with each other, not just with the book. The online presence of bookclubs is something to be investigated. It has been estimated (by the *Guardian*) that there are around 50,000 book clubs active in the UK. There are also telephone book clubs for blind people, who prefer books in Braille to audio books, since they can go at their own pace, and there is also a new machine available for the blind, which translates written text into audio, although it is extremely expensive. There are book clubs for books in Welsh, for all the minority languages in the UK, library book clubs, and of course, the famous Richard & Judy book club which has space online to post reviews and reactions. The magazine *Newbooksmag* is a kind of book club, as there are books which can be had free in every issue if you write in, with people encouraged to write their own reviews. I am sure it is only a matter of time until this magazine goes online.

I think there are several book clubs in Stoke Newington, but N16 Book Club has a MySpace identity – it describes itself as female, a swinger and one hundred years old. It also has definite tastes in literature and seems not to really like people who think they are fashionable. If I had lived in North London, I think I would have tried joining, since they seem to enjoy having a fluid membership and meet in a bar rather than in people's houses. I have always wondered what happens to the hapless spouses of book club members when once or twice a year, ten strangers invade their living rooms and drink their claret.

N16 Book Club's Blurbs

About me:

I am a book club based in Stoke Newington, London.

Who I'd like to meet:

People who quite like books that aren't stupid and rubbish.

1. DO NOT WANT TO MEET PEOPLE WHO HAVE ONLY READ BUKOWSKI AND JOHN FANTE PEOPLE THAT THINK SMALL PRESS TOMES ABOUT RECOVERING ALCOHOLICS WRITTEN BY FAILED MUSICIANS ARE THE HEIGHT OF LITERATURE; PEOPLE THAT THINK ONLY BOOKS WRITTEN IN MORSE CODE ARE INTELLECTUALLY WORTHY

We like things such as: JG Ballard, AM Homes, Jorge Luis Borges, ZZ Packer, David Mitchell, Kevin Brockmeier, Adrian Tomine, Paul Auster, David Foster Wallace, Daniel Clowes, Hilary Mantel, *Middlemarch*, Ian McEwan, Charles Dickens, Raymond Chandler, Patricia Highsmith, Alan Moore, Kathryn Dunn, Geoff Ryman, Martin Amis, Grant Morrison, Dan Rhodes, Gwendoline Riley, Carson Mccullers, Franz Kafka, Sam Lypsite, Jane Austen, Daniel Dennett, A Confederacy of Dunces, George Orwell, Hanif Kureishi, Martin Amis, Kelly Link, Thomas Pynchon, Philip Roth, Haruki Murakami, Damon Runyon, Barry Gifford, Neil Gaiman, Philip K Dick, Aldous Huxley, Truman Capote, Flannery O'Connor, H.G. Wells, Christopher Priest, Steve Aylett, Mark Poirier, Dave Eggers, Zadie Smith.

Book clubs are not just about reading books, they are of course, about social groups, fitting in, and belonging. As an independent publisher, one of the things we pride ourselves on is not fitting in, so it's hardly surprising that none of us in this office is a member of a book club. One for my retirement, I guess.

Catheryn Kilgarriff

Bookselling and the Net Revolution

The role of Amazon

If there is one major commercial organisation which has to be discussed in this book, it must be Amazon. Amazon represents everything that anyone who has spent even a few weeks studying or working in marketing and business will have had rammed down their throats – the first people to start a new business in a field which is as yet undiscovered will collar 80% of the market, leaving all the latecomers scrapping over the remaining 20%.

Of all the online retailers of books, Amazon is the one who gets the most clicks. The main organization that is posing a risk to Amazon is Google – a company not known at the moment for its prowess in putting books into cardboard boxes and delivering them to your door. However, Google is also a company who have managed a 'first' – they are the most popular search engine in the world. Google's intent is in fact to make most of the content of books available for free on the internet – an aim in which it is amply assisted by Wikipedia, who have encouraged people to contribute articles for free on all the subjects, theories, people and companies in existence. If Google and Wikipedia had their way, we would spend all our time online instead of reading books in some quiet corner under the shade of an apple tree. In fact, if e-readers become cheap enough and are able to be read in sun-dappled shadows, perhaps the much heralded end to the book will arrive.

Similarly, 20% of your product, in any field, is supposed to contribute 80% of your revenue. It was to counter arguments like this that the Long Tail Theory was invented by Chris Anderson in 2004, published in an article in *Wired*. The Long Tail Theory refers to an essay by Clay Shirky titled 'Power Laws, Weblogs and Inequality', which noted that a few websites have many links, but the majority of websites only have a few links. This was developed by Chris Anderson into a theory which stated that you could make up a trade to rival that of the largest companies by selling a few of a huge number of different products. Amazon was the prime example as the sale of a huge variety of books in small quantities built a trade which started to challenge that of established bricks and mortar bookshops.

Amazingly, Amazon manages to profit from both of these economic rules, since it is the first point of call for anyone looking for both brand new and backlist books which are unlikely to be found in bookshops. Amazon lead the way in the sale of new books because of a clever device on their site, which rates the interest in a new book. If your Amazon rating goes into the hundreds then you know as the author of a new book that you have probably made it. In contrast, if your book's rating is 480,000, then you definitely are a contributor to the Long Tail Theory, where one or two book sales a year will make the sale of many different titles a worthwhile business for Amazon.

Amazon has many assets which we suspect it doesn't really know about. If we are interested in a new author, perhaps from a different country, whose book we would translate into English we can look on other Amazon sites around the world to see what the rating is, whether there are author reviews and if the books generally look as if they have been published with care. If we find hardly any mention of the book on any Amazon site, we know we are unlikely to do well with it in the English language. Similarly, if an American publisher is interested in selling us a book, then its rating on amazon.com will be crucial in our decision.

One point that must be mentioned here is that reviews on the Amazon sites are frequently written by the author, the author's friends or people who want to be the author's friends. It's a bit like an extension of MySpace. On amazon.com right now there is a review for *EEEEE EEE EEEE* by Tao Lin, which is supposed to be by Jonathan Safran Foer. In fact it is a review for a blender. The joke here is that it still may be a review for Tao Lin's book by Foer, but then again, it might not. Amazon's site is a place where in-jokes can be displayed for all to see, understand or be puzzled by. Reviews on Amazon are rarely more than three paragraphs long, which actually makes them fairly suspect in the first place. You can write a review which says 'This is a really great book' and Amazon will put it up – presumably because this is better than nothing. However, no newspaper would bother publishing a review of this nature. Does this make all reviews on Amazon negligible? I tend to think that the reader can distinguish false reviews from those posted up on the site in a flush of enthusiasm by someone who has just read a book they think is astounding. An easy way to tell is to look at the date when the review was posted: if there is a flurry of reader reviews around the book's publication date then these must be more suspect than one posted six months or a year later. Also, for a publisher who is promoting literature in translation, readers are precious and are able to spread the word about a book through their friends. It would be sad if I was to join the throng of authoritarian forces who claim that only reviews in august journals and literary magazines can be trusted.

The strange business of being involved with writing

The more I think about the issues in this book already, the more I think that the internet manages to make the world of writing smaller and thus more accessible. The differences in thought processes between writers and readers can be seen and understood better when you have interactive correspondence on websites to read, not just the books and reviews in newspapers.

I have mentioned the website of writer Laila Lalami. Recently, her site brought to our attention an article in the *New York Times* magazine about new writers to watch, all of whom are still unpublished. Now, the very act of these writers being in the *New York Times* magazine means that they are already beyond our grasp. But I am glad to be aware of this article. I will probably return to it many times over the coming few years to see if these authors did find publishers and readers. However, if it were not for Lalami's blog I would not have known about this article unless a newspaper or trade paper found it. The feeling of triumph in finding this article before these institutions and journalists find it is also significant, if a little sad on my part. But I do feel connected to the global village of writers and the mysterious forces which decree that a minority achieve stellar success and the majority fall into some vast remainder vat.

Where I become really interested however, is in an entry for May 15th 2007 in which Laila Lalami writes about a recent talk she did in Morocco, for her own book *Hope and Other Dangerous Pursuits:*

> A young woman asked me, 'Your book deals with illegal immigration, fundamentalism, judicial corruption, and so on. Do you think that writing about negative things in Morocco makes your work more attractive to the Western reader?' I must say I was taken aback because I had never thought of my work as being about 'negative things'. I explained that the book describes complex characters, who are put in complex situations. Some of the things in their lives are positive, others are negative. One could just as easily say that, in addition to illegal immigration, for example, the book deals with filial love and romantic love and platonic love, so why not mention those things, too?
>
> I thought that I had laid those concerns about outsider/insider writing to rest. How wrong I was. A smiling young man in the front row asked, 'I found your story "The Fanatic" to be insulting,

in the same way that *Things Fall Apart* by Chinua Achebe was insulting to Nigeria.'

This, of course, wasn't so much a question, as a comment, more specifically a challenge to me to say something for myself. The problem was that I had already forgotten about my book by then because I was trying to get my head wrapped around the idea that *Things Fall Apart* was insulting to Nigeria.

'Have you ever been to Nigeria?' I asked.

'No.'

'How do you know that it's insulting? In what way is it insulting?'

'Because Okonkwo is polygamous and he beats his wives.'

I was mystified as to how this young student could have possibly reduced Achebe's work to this one-liner. The gentleman who had introduced me, a professor in the English department, squirmed in his seat in embarrassment. I spoke about Achebe's work, explained that the book is set in a very specific time and place in Nigerian history, that there is much more to Okonkwo than the polygamy, that the book deals with many issues, most importantly the appearance of British colonialism and how it changes Okonkwo's world.

As I talked, I realised that this young man (and indeed several of the people who were so eager to ask questions that put literature on trial) was not a regular reader of books. It seems impossible to me that anyone who reads novels on a usual basis could come up with such a reductive interpretation, and I felt an overwhelming sadness, for him, and for what he was missing. After the reading, he came up to the podium to have his picture taken with me. I didn't know what to think. I didn't know if he had asked that question because he truly felt the way he said he did, or because he thought it would be funny, or if he was just being a punk. I think what upset me most was this expectation that my work, or literature in general, should be a stage in which good things happen to good people, and bad things happen to bad people. In other words, what this student wanted was a fairytale. Life is not like that, and neither is literature.

The strangest interpretation, however, came when a student asked me: 'In your book, a young woman goes from being a religious conservative who covers her hair to being a prostitute in Spain. Do you think that this is a metaphor for Morocco, which prostitutes itself to the West through the Free Trade Agreement?'

I think I heaved a very audible sigh. Sometimes, a scarf is just a scarf, it's not a symbol for a country. I used as an example the anecdote that Sydney Lumet tells about asking filmmaker Akira Kurosawa why he framed a particular shot in Ran the way he did. Kurosawa's answer was that if the shot had been an inch to the left, a factory would have been exposed, and if it was one inch to the right, the airport would be in the frame, and neither of these buildings belonged in a period movie. The students all had a good laugh.

Posted by Laila Lalami at 12:00am

The reason this post strikes a chord with me is that it is a perfect example of a writer coming across an audience who have a completely different agenda to her own. While Laila Lalami believes she has written a beautiful account of four people trying to leave Morocco by boat, perhaps for a better life, perhaps not, her audience, who probably have little interest in reading her book, have come to the talk determined to air their nationalist pride in Morocco. They use the story line of a devout, headscarf-wearing Muslim who finds herself reduced to prostitution as an insight into the political beliefs of the author, and her thoughts about her country, Morocco, which Lalami obviously did not intend in the slightest. Laila Lalami deals with the politics inferred in this exchange with incredible good humour. One assumes she is a young woman, who may be a Muslim, but who does not wish to live with her head covered and who has not had an overbearing, conservative father or husband demanding that she does this.

I would like to publish more books which deal with the position of women in different societies throughout the world. In many ways, the best time to have been born female is now, since so many of the constrictions, prejudices and problems associated with being female have been lifted. However, I am aware that one of the reasons I believe this is because I work in an office where there is no male authority figure (we do have male members of staff, but we work as a team, and we do not have any problems). But there are obvious differences between Muslim and non-Muslim countries and the fact that a great many Muslim women wish to cover their heads means that while some people regard them as restricting, others see them as trying to make a difference between themselves and women who do not care about being seen by men. If Laila Lalami did not have a blog, she would be unable to deal with the exchange which happened at the talk in Morocco. She has managed to avoid any outburst of anger that her work could be misrepresented so thoroughly. She had added humility and good humour in equal measure, retaining her dignity. But I am in no doubt that she left this talk feeling angry and impotent – if only a story could be just a story.

Catheryn Kilgarriff

Podcasts and the word 'download'

So have recent developments in the net revolution delivered all that they promised? The uniquely convenient experience of accessing podcasts has enabled many readers to gain insight into an author's work through watching video clips of readings or hearing recordings of them speaking about their new books for example. Whilst other formats enable users to download material or watch live footage through a process of streaming, podcasts are digital media files available on the internet that are not in real time, but can be played back on portable devices or users' PCs at their leisure

That, for just a small free, you can listen to Tony Juniper, director of Friends of the Earth, speaking at the Hay Festival in 2007, for example, might tempt you into buying his book *How Many Lightbulbs Does it Take to Change a Planet?* When the speaker is convincing the audience will respond, but of course the opposite holds true also.

Anyone for audiobooks?

There are those prophets of doom who have argued that being able to purchase audiobooks online would further destroy the decreasing market for new books in print, a market already meant to be suffering from competition from e-books since their emergence in the 1990s. To my knowledge there are very few people who would choose an e-book over a 'paper' one (in fact I've yet to meet anyone who has even made use of one) and at this stage of the game neither can the online audiobook be considered a serious rival for anything appearing on the page.

That is not to say that the genre isn't popular, that the self-starters who have launched themselves on the net in glee at the prospect of selling audiobooks in their thousands are not making a success of their enterprises. A quick 'Google' in search of 'online audiobooks' will take you to www.audiobookscorner, www.novelarts.com, and www.audiobooksonline.com. There are sites where you can rent audiobooks, such as www.simplyaudiobooks for example, sites which offer children's books specifically, see www.thekidswindow.com, and all manner of promotions including shock-horror 'FREE!' audiobooks are offered by sites such as www.listen2online.co.uk. But the fact is that this is a specialised market. And whilst many people may be willing to dip into the territory, I don't think it will be bringing about the downfall of Waterstone's just yet.

Thumbs up to the e-book experience?

'But whatever happened to the e-book?' I hear some open-minded publishers cry. And there are those who remain optimistic.

In the *Guardian* recently Andrew Marr writes with nostalgia about the experience of curling up with a good 'old-fashioned' book. However, his parting note that is that the e-book is arriving, softly-softly though it may be.

He begins with some enthusiastic comments about the beauty of a book-as-object, and it's true that there is something truly joyous about opening a book, about fondling its cover, folding back its first pages, settling in your loving hands.

> If you are selling e-books I'm a hard sell[...]my enthusiasm for traditional books is just this side of pervy. I live among mountains of them and always have, among the most beautiful mass-produced objects of all time. Some of my most treasured possessions are broken-backed, scribbled-in, jacketless books first read when a teenager; they've lasted longer than merely human friends[...]They are pleasingly silent and dignified, there when needed, discreet and patient[...]When I eventually become a nasty-minded, dribbling old man I'm sure I will be found creeping round second-hand bookshops, sniffing the produce, snuffling with pleasure.

He's not the only one. I remember a time at Penguin Books (where I once worked) when all the staff were invited department-by-department to witness high tech presentations (well, Powerpoint was new then!) about the e-book, the death of publishing, the new age that 'electronic paper' was about to welcome in. The way we read would be transformed beyond recognition! Not so. As Marr wittily observes in his article, the arrival of the e-book has been more of a 'tortoise progress', than the flash of a digital net frenzy:

> It's partly that traditional books are such good technology, even compared with CDs or newspapers. They are a little larger than the hand, extremely portable, nice to hold and look at and remarkably cheap[...]Simple technology that works is unlikely to go out of fashion.

Literature without books

Perhaps the problem has been that no decent e-book has been developed yet. Users report that they are not as easy on the eyes, it's not as easy to flick through them, and they are not as easily portable.

In a trial he describes as 'bibliophile, or perhaps bibliomanic meets book-killer', Marr tested out the new iRex Iliad (no product placement here, I swear – the Sony Reader is as good a gadget also apparently!) and was pleasantly surprised. Perhaps it was the fact that it was clothed in leather, resembling a slender filofax or – dare we say it – book?! Perhaps it was the fact that this tool could be used to transport newspapers and work notes as well as novels or poetry. Perhaps it was the first e-book he had come across where the screen could be easily read in daylight. In any case, soon he was if not converted, then at least considering the e-book as something he might use in the future.

> For me, the most important moment came reading a Sherlock Holmes story when I suddenly realised I'd been following the tale for several minutes having completely forgotten about the Iliad itself. This, of course, is essential: how many of us could get anything out of a book if we were constantly saying, in a small voice, 'Hey, look at me – I'm reading this thing'?

The important questions will be how much can you store on one of these things, how easy can you turn pages, is it worth forking out a few hundred pounds for one? It may not look as if the e-book is going to replace book-buying *ordinaire* anytime soon, but perhaps it will make some headway in the market after all, especially with the environmentally conscious welcoming another gadget that will cut down on the amount of paper that we shift around, some argue needlessly...

The good, the great and...Google

Suppose the e-book does experience a revival with these new models from Sony Reader and the iRex Iliad appearing on the market. Who will lead the way in orchestrating downloads? Do we need to even ask this question? There are many who believe that the-giant-that-is-Google will not only enable the e-book to become a regular fixture on the book buying market, but will in fact create the market.

> The iPod has done it with music, Flickr has done it with photos, MySpace has done it with bands and Saatchi is doing it with paintings. The question is: can Google do the same thing with books by creating an international online market place for them enabling readers to download volumes in their entirety – at a price of course – to their iPods, Blackberrys or smartphones? (Vic Keegan writing for the *Guardian*, 2007)

Google hasn't easily wiped rivals off the board in other areas. Googlemail has yet to rival Microsoft's hotmail in terms of user numbers (and this is despite the fact that it is commonly acknowledged to offer a better system). The Google video subsidiary couldn't achieve market dominance on its own so Google bought the hugely popular video clips site YouTube. However, with reading matter the situation is slightly different.

At the moment, in order to include titles that are currently in print, Google would only have to do deals with a relatively small amount of publishers, rather than millions of individuals. As

Vic Keegan notes in the *Guardian*, this means that 'Google, with its capacity to scan a huge number of books, ought to be in an advantageous position.' However, with the huge number of books that are out of print and which could be resurrected through the new print-on-demand presses, new companies may emerge that could overtake Google's apparent supremacy. Following the millions of readers in Japan who are already familiar with the experience of reading entire novels they have downloaded onto their phone screens,Vic Keegan tried out i-cue.co.uk, which offers such novel presentation as one word flashing onto your screen at a time. Though reluctant to cast his vote in favour, Keegan joins the troupes who believe this 'eerily addictive way of killing time on the tube' may yet take off:

> Reading from a digital device will never compare to the pleasure got from reading a real book – but that doesn't mean there won't be a huge market for online books as the digital revolution rolls on.

Virtual book tours

Regardless of the effect that e-books and the Google factor may have on book sales, there will always be innovative ideas that involve an alternative approach to the promotion of books and one that I am particularly taken with is the 'virtual book tour'.

There is something inherently amusing about the idea of an author going on a promotional tour without leaving the comfort of their couch. As a member of a variety of bands, I am no stranger to sleeping on railway station platforms in the name of good gigs and I can't think why more musicians aren't going for this 'virtual tour' business. What a fantastic way to put yourself about a bit!

For example, a recent Marion Boyars title on the new craft movement, *The Crafter Culture Handbook* by Amy Spencer, enjoyed a huge amount of support from online crafting communities eager to contribute ideas and come along to the launch, as well as telling their friends, colleagues and fellow crafters about the book. As many of the individuals running craft-sites are also contributors to magazines about crafting, Spencer was able to get online reviews and print reviews for the title through a little online networking. But do these virtual book tours translate into sales in a similar fashion, when the literary networks in question aren't necessarily so mutually supportive of each other's efforts as the crafters are?

For an idea of what a virtual book tour might involve, here is the timetable that US author Francis Ray undertook recently in her quest for publicity for a new novel, *Dreaming of You*.

RomanceJunkies.com host online chat with Francis Ray, Sunday, September 10th 2006 at 9pm EST

Join RomanceJunkies.com Sunday evening, September 10pm, 2006 at 9pm EST/ 8 pm CST, as they chat with national bestselling author, Francis Ray about her new release, *Dreaming of You*. The chat will be held via their online community at this link – www.romancejunkies.com/chat.html.

Mark your calendar and plan to join us!

Delores 'Queen of Promotion' Thornton puts *Dreaming of You* in the Author Spotlight at BlackRefer.com! September 6th 2006

The *Dreaming of You* Virtual Book Tour is travelling the Information Highway again and our next stop is for BlackRefer.com where Delores 'Queen of Promotion' Thornton's review of *Dreaming of You* makes the Author Spotlight!

Delores Thornton, founder of Marguerite Press and Marguerite Press Promo, is the 'Literary Expert' at BlackRefer.com.

BlackRefer.com, founded in June of 2002, is a unique human-compiled online directory consisting of some of the most popular and hard-to-find Black websites today. Visit Blackrefer.com today!

The Black Butterfly Review Group gives *Dreaming of You* 5-out-of-5 Flutters!
August 30th 2006
Dreaming of You is finally in stores and the reviews are rolling in. So our next virtual tour stop will be to visit the Black Butterfly Review website where Eleanor Shields, founder, gives this third Grayson family saga a perfect score – 5-out-of-5 flutters!

AllBooks Review highly recommends *Dreaming of You!*
August 28th 2006
Our next stop on the *Dreaming of You* Virtual Tour is for AllBookReviews.com where Nancy Morris reviewed *Dreaming of You* and highly recommends it to their online community!

New Release Chat with Francis Ray, Friday, August 25th 2006 at 8pm EST
August 25th 2006
Join the Romance Design Community as they chat with Francis Ray about her upcoming release, *Dreaming of You* on Friday evening, August 25th 2006 at 8pm EST. The chat will be held in their Community Chatroom at this link: http://www.romancedesigns.com/chatroom.cfm.

Mark your calendar and plan to join us!

August 24th 2006
The next stop on our *Dreaming of You* Virtual Book Tour is *Romance At Heart* Magazine.

August 23rd 2006
Our *Dreaming of You* Virtual Book Tour will be making a stop this evening, August 23rd, 2006 to join Ms Toni Bonita and the Sexy Ebony BBW African American Book Club as they chat with Francis about her last novel, *Any Rich Man Will Do* and of course about her soon to be released Grayson Romance Novel,

> *Dreaming of You*!
>
> The chat will begin promptly at 9pm EST/ 8pm CST and will take place in the club's chatroom. So please mark your calendars and PDAs and join us!

The idea of the virtual book tour is taking off. For example, US writer and self-proclaimed 'hype hag' Karin Gillespie has launched her own informal Girlfriend Cyber Circuit, a group made up of twenty-one female writers with blogs, each of whom agrees to host and publicise two or three fellow 'girlfriends' a month to bump up sales and name recognition. Gillespie admits that she doesn't always love the books she endorses on her site but says, 'I would never say if I didn't like something!' (from the *Village Voice*).

Rebecca Gillieron

Freedom and immediacy

The main advantage of writing and publishing on the internet is that it is immediate. Although no one may look or read what you have written, an author can be sure that their work is available to be enjoyed by others.

One of the saddest things about being a publisher is that we spend most of our time being negative to people and rejecting work. I decided early on not to give reasons for this, since often there really is no polite way of saying that the writer's vision just does not coincide with my own view of how a piece of writing should turn out. Every individual has different tastes and someone who is going to experiment by printing 2,000 copies of a book when they have no idea if anyone will want to pay for the pleasure of reading it, well, that person just has to have enjoyed reading it in the first instance. If the passion and magic does not happen, then it is best left alone.

Prior to the internet, if an author could not persuade a publisher to print their work, the only course open to them was to arrange private or public readings. The 60s were full of poets declaiming their work in pubs, and actually, at Hay Festival in 2007, there was an author in the street performing his work. He had CDs of his poems for sale, with large signs saying 'NOT SUITABLE FOR CHILDREN.' Perhaps he thought this would encourage buyers. Now, authors can tap away into their computers late at night, getting carried away and check the next day that it is online at whatever website they have posted it on. There are even websites set up simply for authors to exhibit their work for it to be then critiqued by their fellows. One example is the frontlist.com. I am supposed to receive emails when a well critiqued piece of writing in the genres I am interested in appears, so I can consider publishing it. I have had a look on the site a few times, and I am actually surprised that there are not a huge amount of submissions on it. Perhaps word spreads slower through writers' ranks than it does through publishers' arteries. Publishers' blogs, newsletters and such like are extremely effective in communicating with their core audience which is other people involved in the book trade.

The disadvantages of a small world getting smaller...

If the internet means that thought, debate, issues and controversy travel faster than they would if we were limited to printed media, then it also means that there is not so much left to chance discoveries. It's just too easy to have access to other people's thought processes.

When you start to read a book, there is often a period of time at the beginning where you are unsure if you like it or not. I recently went to see Martin Amis at the Hay Festival. I am one of those people who picked up on a misogynist tendency in Martin Amis. It didn't really bother me but I just felt that he did not like women. As one of them, I felt there were plenty of other writers I would prefer to spend my time reading but I did notice that my view was not shared by my husband, who has assiduously bought every Martin Amis book ever written. While on holiday in Turkey a few years ago, said husband had brought with him a copy of Amis's *Experience*. This is a long book – over 500 pages – and it covers every stage of his life, from failure at school to academic success, step-mothers, neighbours and famous friends. You can guess my response – I finally started to know and understand the man behind the posing of his early novels and liked it. My only regret was that the glue on the spine could not stand up to the Turkish heat and our copy disintegrated beyond the point at which I could ever ask Martin Amis to sign it.

Martin Amis said many things at Hay, including that he did not understand the relevance of poetry in the 20th century, since no one had the time to savour pure feelings, or phrases. He also commented on how strange odd stanzas of poetry looked when printed in review sections of newspapers, alone in boxes in the middle of a page. This is a feeling I have often shared – I sometimes force myself to read the poem against my will because I know it will be good for my soul. Unwisely, Amis went on to say that poetry was dead with a 'ghoulish afterlife in the form of tours, readings, poetry slams and all the rest of it.' Amis's view was immediately rubbished in the *Guardian* (both online and in print) a week later by Tishani Doshi and others, thus showing that you have to be prepared for any reaction. Although you yourself have no idea who is in the audience at Hay, you can be sure that they are all listening acutely to your opinions.

So, the next fine day I went to our bookshelves and found *A House of Meetings*, which is Martin Amis's most recent short novel. And I am not sure if I like it or not after reading fifty pages. I went to look at the reviews which can be found online and found that quite a few people who had read the book all the way through were still not sure if they liked it or not. So I will just have to read it to the end in the hope that there are more passages I like than ones I do not (I did spot the word misogynist in the book, so obviously Amis is aware of the existence of people like me amongst his readers, which I find quite interesting. Perhaps he is one writer who would really like to have the chance of experiencing life as a member of the opposite sex, since he seems to find women difficult to understand.) And my final word on poetry – well, I think that there are many places where poetry is essential, for example when looking at Tintern Abbey, when listening to bad lyrics, followed by good lyrics, and when comparing the literary voices of different centuries, the poets seem to have the ability to perfectly capture the mood of their time. I do agree that newspaper editors who slavishly labour to include poetry as 10% of their literary content are fighting a losing battle. It's all too obvious to succeed. This debate shows us how the same subject can move from a live audience, to the printed word, and then onto the internet.

So, if it is possible to easily access most of the reviews that have ever been written about a book when you are halfway through a book and undecided, does the internet have too much sway in book buying decisions? Could the internet be another kind of overwhelming force, where many different sites all start to recommend the same book, much in the way that the same books all seem to be reviewed by the papers at the same time. Are we too governed by other people's opinions? On the Book Depository website, in the interview about Serpent's Tail publishing house, Pete Ayrton talks about the 'cultural gatekeepers' that independent publishers have to get through – the critics in the press and the buyers in the chains – in order for their books to be seen on sale in the shops. He is thankful that word of mouth – both online and in person, makes up in literary enthusiasm for the obstacles that these gate-keepers often put in the way of books which do not follow the mainstream. The online word of mouth is the new channel, and hopefully, one that will grow in strength as time goes by.

The future

What will the world of bookselling and book blogs be like in five years time? Five years ago, no one in the UK would have predicted the growth of discounting in book sales, the growth of one chain, Waterstone's, to such an extent that Borders has recently put itself up for sale. On the publishing side, this has been mirrored by the development of eight or so large publishing conglomerates who continue to expand in size and influence. It is harder than ever to survive as an independent press since they cannot compete on advances, marketing spend, or any number of factors. Where they can compete though, is on the flexibility of their staff, who tend to be extremely computer literate and highly educated. They are often skilled at using marketing techniques which do not rely on advertising agencies and the sides of buses. Small presses can usually bring out books quickly, and design is a marketing skill which is available to all small publishers who are willing to employ new graduates in illustration and graphics, most of whom are very keen for work.

People would have predicted the growth in internet sales. Sales at Amazon are increasing at the rate of 15–18% annually, although this includes DVDs, while sales at large chains like Barnes & Noble in the US are only achieving 2% gains, or actually falling. There is one huge difference between the US and UK book trade rules of trade. In the US, books can be returned at any time, while in the UK they can only be returned three months after they were supplied, and up to nine months after this date, so within a calendar year. This means that after one year, publishers can refuse to accept return requests, while in the US, returns can appear at any time and the only way to stop them is to put a title out of print. As you can imagine, publishers rarely do this, as it is a total admission of failure, not to mention a rather depressing course of action, for both publisher and author.

So, if the internet is the one avenue for trade in which it is acknowledged that there is rapid growth, one would assume that the development of trusted book evaluation sites would also increase. Will we see a site like Readysteadybook being bought by Amazon? Its sister company, The Book Depository, which runs part of its book sales organisation through Amazon Marketplace, is already run by ex-Amazon employees, so it would seem extremely likely. Mark Thwaite, who as we have seen writes book reviews for The Book Depository and runs Readysteadybook, has a maverick, independent mind, who likes literature in translation and independent presses so his interests run counter to those of the large conglomerates. At the moment, I think it would make the team at The Book Depository throw up their hands in horror at the thought of Amazon swallowing them like a mid-morning snack. However, we have seen smaller web businesses in other fields, travel, social networking, broadband supply etc, bought up by larger ones, and I am sure that Amazon are aware that The Book Depository is growing, and is a potential rival for online sales. The fact that The Book Depository favours the independent presses, and encourages the 'long tail' (our backlist sells well through The Book Depository), is something which, when the right time comes, will not deter Amazon. They will want to retain their supremacy as the first online vendor of books. Of course, there would be nothing to prevent the owners of The Book Depository and Readysteadybook setting up a new, more maverick book review and bookselling website if Amazon should decide to descend with an offer they could not refuse. In the world of publishing, we have seen many smaller houses swallowed up by larger ones, only to see their founder then leave and set up smaller concerns.

So, is there a growing link between book review websites and book retailing sites, of which The Book Depository is the first major player? Will waterstones.com, barnesandnoble.com and amazon.com start employing book reviewers? Or do they know that since in this form – on a book selling site – reviews most definitely will influence sales, it is far too risky a strategy. While reviews on Amazon are submitted by eager enthusiasts, it is easy to dismiss them as unauthorised, faulty and not to be trusted. However, imagine if the Poet Laureate was the main fiction reviewer for Amazon – a not wholly unlikely scenario – then of course, he would have real credibility and the sales of books on Amazon would climb inexoriably higher for books he liked, while they would slump for books he did not enjoy.

For this reason, it is quite important that independent publishers develop websites where they sell to the public, with reviews available – both from major newspapers and from online specialists. If the public becomes accustomed to buying books online from a multitude of sites, then there will be no possibility that the baton of power is passed from bookselling giants to online giants. Since books are written by people from all walks of life and in all subjects, it is surely fair that they are sold by a huge variety of people. I would like to see more authors selling their books and most publishers would be happy to give them trade discounts so this was profitable for all. An explosion in the availability of books from a huge variety of online sites is what is needed to stop the rise of super web companies.

The US: market leader in online communications

The first website with considerable content on books I became aware of was Salon.com. It came from the US, and instantly assumed a glamourous aura, with a reputation for intellectual prowess and choosiness over what articles appeared.

Salon.com has ten subject areas, including News, Politics, Tech and Business. This is not just a book review site – it's a portal which hoped to become a dot com success. Salon.com was set up as a business but it appears to have lost massive sums of money in its short history. The stock now hovers at just over one US dollar per share and it makes its money from advertising, its premium service and syndication of articles. It's a superior online magazine, using the best writers, and accolades for its authors. One of them, Laura Miller, has been compared to Pauline Kael, thus becoming a respected book critic. Her book, *The Salon.com Reader's Guide to Contemporary Authors* is one of the best books of lists available.

Salon.com is very different from the enthusiastic outpourings of the voluntarily maintained sites this book is mainly concerned with. I find it hard to understand how a dot com company managing to lose over one million US dollars every year is still in existence. Perhaps the investors are very patient people and expect the company to find new ways of generating profit online. However, unless Salon.com turns itself into an innovative publishing house, which I am sure is not beyond its talents, I cannot really see how it can compete with the online news channels owned by the major TV and radio news corporations.

If Salon.com had come into existence five years later, perhaps it would not have been set up as a major information portal, hoping to compete with CNN.com or bbc.co.uk for up-to-date information on all the major issues. It could have been set up as a contemplative site with no need to generate huge sums of cash in order to keep up with the joneses of online information.

It may be helpful to take a look at the whole dot com phenomenon. In the 1980s, all over the world, the first online entrepreneurs started to make themselves heard. Some became incredibly famous. Boo.com in Sweden was an online retailer of fashion. Its owners, the Swedish Ernst Malmsten, Kajsa Leander and Patrik Hedelin, apparently got through $120 million of start-up capital. Their parties and launches were almost more famous than the site. It was also the case that the site was difficult to buy off, so many people found that they could not further their transactions and successfully pay for items. As fashion is mainly an impulse buy, this must have had immediate and disastrous consequences. As in all things computer based, the technology has improved hugely as time has gone by and computers and programmes which would have cost many thousands of dollars can now be bought for hundreds. This office existed for three years with one Apple computer, a powerful G3, which we took in turns to use. For the last two years though, there have always been a couple of computers which are not being used, and our capacity to produce good design and marketing, as well as on-screen editing, has meant that we are able to produce more books per year. We can also sell them ourselves online through our website. In the 1990s, these aims were simply pipe dreams.

The Swedish people were far from enamoured by the famous dot com stars and I heard that became unwelcome at fashionable parties in Sweden since it was thought that they brought ill repute to the country.

Dot com companies are loved and hated by the press in equal measure. Since technology failures can be gleefully reported in the press and they tend to affect thousands of people simultaneously, they make good news copy. Everyone can recall times when the automated banking system crashed on pay day with thousands of people going overdrawn as their mortgages and other payments went out of their accounts before their salaries went in. On holidays and near Christmas there are often reports of dot com technology failing or the unavailability of the latest prized electronic toy. The other famous failing is for companies to make pricing mistakes on their websites, then being forced to honour thousands of orders for underpriced stock. News.com ran the following story in November 2000, at a time when the dot com boom was at its height, and you might have thought that the press would be praising the efforts of new companies to change the way we traded.

> Friday morning, Amazon suffered a thirty minute outage, and BestBuy suffered periodic outages from Thursday night through Sunday.

One reason for BestBuy's troubles was the rumor that it would begin selling the much-hyped and hard-to-find PlayStation 2 video game player, according to spokeswoman Laurie Bauer. Customers were also trying to get information about a special promotion the Minneapolis, Minn.-based company had advertised.

'Those two things gave us much more traffic than we expected,' Bauer said. 'We've had intermittent (outages)...and the site was very slow.'

About 1.3 million people logged onto Amazon on Friday, according to traffic tracking site Nielsen/NetRatings. But spokesman Bill Curry said the glitch was unrelated.

'It was an internal bug that we caught and squashed,' he said, adding that after the glitch was corrected, Amazon's site suffered no performance problems.

So far, most e-commerce sites have stood up well to holiday traffic, research firm Keynote Systems said. BestBuy.com only launched its site this summer, and this is their first taste of the holiday shopping crunch.

But holiday outages have become commonplace enough and appear to indicate that even with loads of preparation and experience, online stores are still vulnerable to spikes in traffic.

'This time period is especially critical for all these websites,' said Daniel Todd, chief technologist of public services for Keynote. 'This is how they define their success.'

Last Monday, Walmart.com slowed to a crawl, and for about an hour, it took an average of 260 seconds to download, according to Keynote. Visitors can normally download the page in about 3 seconds to 4 seconds, Todd said.

Last week, home grocer Webvan ran out of holiday goodies days before Thanksgiving.

Sites have also gone black as a result of shoppers flocking to online stores during sales or promotions.

Despite that, more people are shopping online: Online purchases from July to September jumped 15.3% from the second quarter to $6.37 billion, the-commerce Department said Monday.

Outages or slow websites can exact a high price. Delays in service can frustrate shoppers, which means people may go elsewhere to buy.

'It's the nature of tech: things break,' Todd said.

Broken-down websites have practically become an online holiday tradition. Shoppers pouring into websites have in the past crippled such online stores as Toysrus.com, Dell Computer, eBay and Virgin Megastore.

Amazon's Curry said that too much is made of the outages. They happen infrequently and usually are fixed quickly.

'It's a reality of most businesses that glitches sometimes occur,' Curry said. 'These problems are aberrations, and whether it's a late airplane flight, or a computer freezing up, they occur. These are very large, complex systems. Over time, we keep getting better at preventing glitches, but inevitably interruptions can occur.'

The challenges for retailers aren't just technical. Earlier this month, a group of Amazon workers announced that they are trying to unionise. Seeking better pay and job security, the workers in the company's Seattle headquarters are attempting to organize their customer service centre employees and affiliations with the Communications Workers of America.

Amazon chief executive Jeff Bezos said recently that there was no need for unions at the company and that union efforts would not disrupt the company's holiday season.

'There are not going to be any interruptions this Christmas,' Bezos said.

The growth of social networking websites is a phenomenon which has gained popularity with the young, teenage users of the internet. However, these sites have not gone unnoticed by the major media players. For example, MySpace is now owned by Rupert Murdoch who also owns News International, and many other media groups, operating from Australia and the UK. So far, the users of MySpace have not abandoned the formula, mainly because it is still free at the point of use. MySpace is the third most popular website in America.

When MySpace was set up, it targeted the creative, musical communities in Los Angeles, photographers and in particular, musicians. Giving musicians the ability to promote their appearances, to upload music to the site, and to spread word of their gigs through adding friends to the site, this meant that bands did not need to find traditional recording companies in order to be heard. The bands were free to make money from their appearances without being owned by a record label, and so two industries were mutually benefiting from the set up – the internet entrepreneurs found ways to have 20,000 people visit a site, to find out about a show, and thus sell advertising and the bands were able to generate audiences for their music.

DeWolfe and Anderson (the supposed founders of myspace – see earlier) announce being part of News Corp will not put off their young members and they believe that working with a major media organisation will bring them power and money, thus enabling them to do more creative things with their site. However, when a corporation has, so the story goes, paid them $580 million essentially for a collection of hobbies, tunes and chatter from a huge number of teenagers who do not have a great deal of disposable income, you have to admire their business acumen. There is further controversy over the acquisition. Another one of the publically-named 'founders', Brad Greenspan, thinks the price of $580 million was too low, because in the year since News Corp bought MySpace, its value has grown by $12 billion. I really don't understand how anyone calculates these figures, since nothing tangible is being traded here. How anyone can value the worth of people looking at an advertising banner and ignoring it is beyond me.

Catheryn Kilgarriff

Bloggers rage against the trade

In earlier chapters it emerged that bloggers' online publishing activities are often a direct response to the shortcomings they feel are typical of mainstream publishers. But it is not only the publishing houses that are facing an online attack. Booksellers, both of the 'real' and internet variety are facing criticism from an inordinate number of book bloggers, all disgruntled that the experience of book-shopping simply doesn't measure up to expectations. Book buying is not just a casual pastime for these people, it is essential to health, happiness and life itself.

So what makes a good bookstore?

At themillionsblog.com, created in 2003 by Max McGee in Philadelphia, a recent post contemplates the advantages that the chains offer – which apparently boil down to comfortable sofas, hot coffee and late opening hours with no one getting sniffy about the amount of time you spend in store – compared to the infinitely preferable independents. In a missive delivered April 20th 2004 and titled 'What Makes a Good Bookstore?' McGee realises that it is this very safeness, this predictability, that is their undoing.

> And therein lies the problem with the chains, they are designed not to surprise you. Their displays will, as decreed from the home office, contain a calculated mix of bestsellers assembled from the major lists. The information that they disseminate is predetermined by prevailing tastes; they are not, themselves, tastemakers. And yet, if there is any more important generator of tastes, trends and shared knowledge in the commercial world than the bookstore, then I don't know about it. Nonetheless, there are very few bookstores that serve this purpose.

The main gripe here is that bookstores shouldn't display only bestselling books but important books also. Since when did UK glamour girl Jordan's autobiography affect the way any of us live our lives? I've nothing against Jordan – who can fail to be impressed by the sales figures of her previous book when the girl barely pens a word herself? The point is that bestsellers of this ilk hardly change the way we think. They serve a purpose, to entertain, but (at the risk of repeating a well-worn objection – let's keep this quick...) they should not be given precedence over more worthy publications.

Fully aware of this danger, the post on themillionsblog.com therefore continues:

> ...one should be able to walk into the bookstore and be able to grasp, based upon which books are on display and based upon conversations with staff and fellow customers, what matters at that moment both in the wider world and in the neighbourhood, from Presidential exposes to burgeoning local talent. At a good bookstore you can place your confidence in the people who run the place.
>
> At Barnes & Noble you can get any book you want if you can find it in the vast fluorescent retail gymnasium, but at a good indie, the kindly book clerk will take his favourite book off the shelf and hand it to you, as if a gift. Most cities of any size have at least one of these good bookstores, and thanks to some recommendations that I have already received, I'm confident that I'll find what I'm looking for in Chicago.

And, just for the record, contributors to themillionsblog.com include bloggers Andrew Saikali in Toronto, Emre Parker in Chicago, Patrick Brown in LA, Emily Colette Wilkinson in California and Noah Deutsch and Gareth Risk Hallberg in Brooklin – and the site is definitely worth browsing.

Blaming the chains

This side of the globe, Ms Baroque in Hackney (encountered briefly in the section on pseudonyms) rants also against the policies of the chains; though in this case the targets are specific and the duality of demons that is Waterstone's and Borders must bear the brunt of her amusing-to-read vitriol.

> **Posted by Ms Baroque at 10:41am on March 29th 2007**
> **A patch-up of a post**
> The blogosphere is humming with all kinds of bad news for writers...Waterstone's, already swallowed alive by HMV, is to be further constricted within the giant gut, shops shut, lists constrained, and 'academic' books (ie, I think, poetry) to be thrown overboard. (It's my metaphor, I can do what I like. A pirate's life for me, yo ho!) Borders is on its way out – well, the parent company wants to concentrate on its domestic market, which means our UK branches (so good for periodicals and American editions) will have to sink or swim as they may; but I think I heard a rumour now of a bailout.
>
> Now, against all that, the Tart of Fiction has been running a very useful series of posts, with many links, about the increasingly surreal way in which publishing today commodifies writers. Susan Hill has also touched on the subject, in fact beating me to my conclusion – which is that the tide has got to turn, sailors must be spat out of whales, albatrosses go home to roost, etc. In short, small presses and booksellers, this is your moment!

Not content with this call to arms, as well as commenting on other, less than welcome, developments within the bookselling industry, Ms Baroque goes on to mock the chains' centralised buying schemes which assume that readers will just buy what is placed before their noses:

> ...I think the corollary to all this has got to be the demise of the high street bookselling giants. I was working in bookselling at the time they started bestriding the land, and everybody predicted dire things. Then the end of the New Book Agreement. Everybody predicted dire things but the industry went, oh no! See! It's making skinflints who never bought books before buy books! It's a bookselling renaissance! Well, what it's done is to take Peter Mayer's dictum about selling books being just like selling carrots and grow it (like a carrot in a polytunnel?) into a monster. The profit margins are gone. Books have got to sell – new bookstores have got to be profitable in their first quarter of trading. Buying is centralised so there is little of the old 'local author, local shop' ethos. We, the punters (okay, not you and me, but our non-writer friends) just buy what's put in front of us, we like those little 'staff recommends' cards – we're not thinking, 'Hey, what's missing?' (Eureka!)

The question is, will the book-buying public swallow such blatant and frankly dull tactics for much longer? Or, as Ms Baroque optimistically predicts, once the novelty of Costa Coffee whilst you browse wears thin, will we all be returning to our local, independent, SMALL bookstores in joyous droves?

> Waterstone's policies have driven a lot of this. I read somewhere recently (but couldn't find it again, so not sure where) that Waterstone's has two out of every three high street book sales. That pretty much means that anyone reading anything off the beaten track (read: not bestseller or 'classic') is not getting it at their local bookshop. I buy a lot in my (remaining) local second-hand shop and otherwise rely utterly on Abe and Amazon. Sadly. This isn't sustainable. Someday soon the bookselling disaster and the publishing disaster will have to come together to be seen as one great big disaster. Independent presses are on the up. Susan Hill is right, and given the whole publishing scene I'm not sure why more isn't being made of this – it is an opportunity for

independent booksellers to rise again and hit back at Waterstone's. (Speaking of small presses, one of the best small presses I know, which has achieved great things already, is run in his off-hours by one guy who works – guess where – in a Waterstone's!)

Of course not all booksellers are 'evil capitalists' who've long forgotten the literary vision of their youth. A number of worthy independents have been mentioned already but I'd just like to mention a particular individual in the US who's personal mission cannot fail to strike a chord. Following *Publishers Weekly* and *The Boston Globe*'s coverage, mediabistro.com picked up the story of twenty-four year old bookseller Alex Green, who last year took it upon himself to sell the entire print run of a title called *Who By Fire, Who By Blood* which US publishers had failed to pick up:

Indie Tries to Sell Out Small Press Print Run

...Why the urgency? Because the novel, which follows Papernick's short story collection *The Ascent of Eli Israel,* is slated for publication by Canadian-based Exile Books – no American publisher wanted the book. Exile, being a small press, can only do so much promotion to make a profit and so Green, proprietor of Back Pages Books, has taken it upon himself to sell out the entire 1,000 copy print run of the book.

If I can prove to a publisher that a 1,000-square-foot bookstore in a suburb of Boston can presell an entire print run before it's released, then maybe American publishers will take a second look,' said Green of what he terms the 1001 Book Project. 'Maybe they look at it and say that maybe if 1,000 people want [a book] from this small bookstore, then maybe thousands of people across the country will buy it.

Between May and June 2006, Back Pages managed to presell more than 230 copies, with another hundred or so sold in Canada and Green said he's heard from readers as far away as Washington DC. I'm not sure whether the book ended up getting a publisher, but I admire Green's attitude: 'We have nothing to lose.' If only more booksellers would go to such lengths to promote a title they believe in – or even ordered a few more copies and actually put them out on the shelves...

Online bookshopping – does it fare any better with the bloggers?

There are one or two book bloggers who dedicate themselves entirely to the evaluation of online bookselling. The aptly titled (or 'unimaginatively titled', depending on whether you're a glass half-full or half-empty kind of person) 'Bookselling Online Blog' is one such site. With categories including Amazon, Barnes & Noble, Alibris (second-hand, rare and out-of-print titles) and Abebooks (whose No 1 seller in May 2007 was the one dollar copy of F Scott Fitzgerald's *The Great Gatsby*, which I find surprising); alongside posts such as that of June 29th 2007 on Amazon's decision to digitise rare and collectable books to be sold online; or posts questioning whether booksellers are affected by Ebay and Google's rivalry online; there's a lot to choose from. And even some more personal advice from the customers themselves, one book buyer for example finds the jacket of a recent purchase (mentioning no names, sadly!) did not match the book inside. Any of you publishers out there got anything you care to admit?

Perhaps it is telling that on a site like this it is still the big names that are getting the recommendations. Of course the Book Depository ('...founded in 2004 with the aim of making "All books available to All" through pioneering supply chain initiatives, republishing and digitising of content') is becoming an increasingly attractive alternative for book buyers online. Offering particular discounts and books with poor availability they are careful to point out that they are not attempting to compete with the likes of Amazon (which they are not necessarily fans of) and on the website they are not afraid to lay claim to the title of 'fastest growing book distributor in Europe'.

Not all online booksellers can safely herald themselves as the next big breakthrough outfit. On www.spikemagazine.com, for example, Splinters blog criticises online bookseller books.co.uk, which by all accounts does not deliver all it promises.

> With a premium domain name like books.co.uk, I was expecting interesting things from this website. Amazon.com is over a decade old now – buying books on the internet has come a long way and become increasingly sophisticated too. What could books.co.uk bring to the party to makes things even better for online book buyers? The answer is, unfortunately, 'not much'.
>
> Where book sites like The Book Depository have recently launched and immediately established their niche by carrying more titles and offering a more personal shopping experience with editorial choices and content, books.co.uk offers a fairly mediocre books price comparison engine between various online booksellers. It works for both UK and USA shoppers.
>
> This is a nice idea, but it's hardly original – one of the original book comparison engines, bookbrain.co.uk, is still online although it seems half dead, while kelkoo.co.uk offers comparison shopping for virtually every product but its reach for books is quite limited.
>
> As a random example, I tried searching books.co.uk for the book I'm currently reading, James Traub's *The Best Intentions: Kofi Annan and the UN in the Era of American World Power.* I typed in 'the best intentions' and hit search. The book didn't turn up in books.co.uk search, despite being published only four months ago, in November 2006. By comparison, it's the first result on amazon.co.uk for the same search terms.
>
> I tried searching for the book's author, James Traub, thinking it's a fairly unusual name and would come up easily – books.co.uk returned no matches. Finally, I tried searching for 'Kofi Annan' –

and *The Best Intentions* finally appeared on the books.co.uk search.

It's a schoolboy error to not have a comparison search engine able to successfully locate books by the authors and titles. If books.co.uk were aiming solely at the pile-em-high-sell-em-low bestsellers to give customers the absolute rock bottom best price then I could forgive them not being able to find a current affairs book - but the fact the search will find *The Best Intentions* on a search for a secondary term but not its title or author makes it difficult to have any trust in getting quick, useful results from books.co.uk.

The design of the site looks quite sloppy as well...

Rebecca Gillieron

Blogging tools and developing technology

Blogs can be constructed and linked to existing websites using a variety of programmes which can be downloaded over the internet. There is no need to buy software, although some of the options include a monthly fee (around five US dollars) which often includes back up facilities for extra security. However, I doubt this includes every eventuality and I have often read blogger's entries where they say that everything disappeared overnight or the comments tool failed to work, or any number of computer disasters which occur on a regular basis. So I wouldn't hope for complete invulnerability. This is one of the reasons for compiling this book – we are pretty sure that one day in the not too distant future, many of the blogs in this book will no longer be in existence, and some may just be frozen in time, as their owner has moved onto fresh pastures. Some of the most popular and accessible blogging tools are: Blogger.com. Livejournal.com, BloggLiveJournal, Typepad, Movable Type, WordPress, ExpressionEngine, and TextPattern.

I am of the school that thinks that blogging is a great way to keep in contact with people, but it should not replace the activity of creating and selling books, so I do not spend a huge amount of time adding pictures and side bars to the blog on the Marion Boyars website. In time, I am sure it will become more embellished, but I do know that a good many other bloggers have fun adding their favourite book covers to the side of their blog with links to other blog sites. This all part of joining the community of bloggers and it's a good idea. What it also means is that you can see who has been commenting on other people's blogs, and soon you realise that how quickly word can spread in the blogosphere. So the technology and customs of cross fertilisation of blog sites help the authors establish their reputations.

Blogger.com, which has recently been bought by Google, is free to use. You have to open a Google account to maintain your blog, but this is fairly simple – you just add an email address and a password.

Livejournal.com looks to me as if it is one of the most accessible and easy to understand blogging tools and the blogs look far more like professionally designed websites. It is completely free and this is one I would investigate further if you are looking to start a blog. It has a series of aims and supports open access software. It is the site that loads fastest on my computer and I will look into using it for new web ventures we may have in the future. The aims of Livejournal are admirably copyleft:

> **Core Values**
>
> We believe in self-expression, and we provide tools that you can use to communicate with others in immediate and in creative ways. We believe in letting you create your own content and to choose how to express yourself, your thoughts, and your feelings.
>
> We believe in diversity, and we welcome and respect different opinions, different cultures, and different perspectives. LiveJournal brings people of various backgrounds together. We strongly support freedom of expression, and we're committed to helping you share your diversity with others.

> We believe in creativity, and we encourage you to use the features that LiveJournal offers to share the process of creating content with your friends. Whether it's in the form of writing, making userpics, or designing layouts, everyone has something to offer. We want to make it easy for you to share that with the world.
>
> We believe in community, and we know that LiveJournal thrives because of its loyal users. We're committed to incorporating your feedback into our product and technical decisions. We partner and collaborate with the community in order to improve the service for everyone -- from the novice to the expert, and everyone in between.
>
> We believe in privacy, and we make sure to safeguard your innermost thoughts. We provide you with the tools to choose who to share your content with, and we respect the decisions you make. We let you decide how you want to protect your privacy, and we work to build a service that you trust.

Livejournal has free software on its site which you can download and use to import photographs from web applications also allowing you build you blog offline, which may free up your computer to complete other tasks while you tinker with your blog. I think it's a good find, and hope others do also.

Typepad has a small monthly charge, and for this I am sure you are reassured that the blog is held safely on a remote server. I have heard recently that large internet companies are buying up empty space in Arizona, and building vast servers which will hold the internet postings of the millions. Strange, that an essentially invisible concept like the Internet should in fact have to resort to bricks and mortar, although it is at least not prime retail space on the high street.

I have yet to come across a blogging tool which takes more than a few tries to master. You can experiment with headers and different design templates and change the look of your blog periodically to add new visual interest. It is easy to load images onto your blog edits, although I have had trouble adding the lady-with-laptop image on this book cover to our blog header. This is probably just as well, because although I think I can detect a pointed shoe in her profile, she does not look like she is wearing very much.

However, bloggers do report problems with the bells and whistles on their websites. Here is bluestalkingreader on recent problems:

> I know my blog's been loading painfully slowly lately, so I've taken a few steps to try and rectify that problem. After taking a long, hard look at the situation (okay, a five second glance), I think a big part of the problem has been the number of fancy schmancy widgets I've so enjoyed having on my sidebars. Those take a lot of blog energy to load, or blogergy, we'll call it, so we sound all hip and smarticle.
>
> The problem is, I take childish delight in widgets, things that dance and flash and look all pretty and animated-y. I sit here clapping my hands and giggling when the pretty lights flash. A sad image, but you may understand more about that once you realise this is coming from someone who firmly believes the people in TV shows are really INSIDE THE TV.
>
> I'm sorry, it just doesn't make sense any other way.
>
> So, out of love for all of you, I've made the ultimate sacrifice and taken off a lot of those way cool widgets. Goodbye, Nerd Detector! So long, Horoscope of the Day... sniff... I've winnowed down to the necessities, and I hope my blog will load all the faster for it. If it doesn't, and you're still having problems, just let me know. There may be something else I can eliminate so things run more smoothly and load more quickly. Yes, I'd do that for you! I know, it's touching, like an episode of Lassie.
>
> If you'll excuse me, speaking of Lassie, I think she just left a mess inside my TV, so I'd better go take care of that.
>
> Sincerely,
>
> The 'maintenance crew' at BSR.

So, it's a case of experimenting with the free software which is there on the internet, looking at blogs which you admire and seeing if you would like to emulate them, and maybe just trying one or two different templates before you launch. Since a blog can be created and placed up in the ether in under five minutes, perhaps the best advice this book can offer is to take things at a slightly slower pace, and work out over a couple of weeks which package is right for what you wish to do with your blog.

The final word on blogs and their impact

In conclusion, what can we say has changed dramatically in the world of books now that the book bloggers have joined the community? It is still the case that the book industry is dominated by a few large publishing corporations, the book headlines are still in love with stories that have little to do with the content of new books (right now there are many columns concerned with the size of advance Tony Blair will command for his memoirs), and columnists enjoy speculating that the recent stock market melt down will mean the end of leveraged takeovers and huge advances to footballers for their well considered autobiographies at the ripe old age of twenty-three. All this is many miles from the literary and artistic concerns of the people we have covered in this book. But this small group of committed individuals can and do make their voices known, read and heard, something which is a small triumph in itself.

I would like to see the voices of the book bloggers heard even louder. I think there is a major problem, despite the pages on feverish comment on literary prizes, radio shows, interviews and profiles, in that the media manages to talk about books in a way that goes over the heads of the vast majority of people. The book bloggers have developed loyal audiences, and I compare them most closely to newspaper columnists who may be your favourite to read each week in the Sunday paper. You get to know a personality and a style, and you find nuggets of new information each week, which makes you go back the following week for more. The book bloggers have another twist which makes them more loveable – they write their thoughts for free. What if a few of the best could be persuaded to write review columns in the book review pages, as an extension of their blogs, writing out of enthusiasm and love for a subject and choosing the books they cover on their own, with no dictates from on high and without receiving payment? This is a radical proposal which would only find acceptance from the world of blogging. As bloggers are known to publishers, they already have access to review copies, which publishers can choose to send, or not send, if they think they are being asked for no purpose other than the blogger would like another nice, shiny book on their coffee table.

There has to be a way of encouraging the reading of books which is more democratic, fair and not full of intellectual concerns that put people off. I know the arguments about the Italians and French being unafraid of discussing philosophy at dinner parties, while the English are only happy on the golf course, but I think it does not have to be this way. Many people have enjoyed reading as children, and somehow they become lost in the plethora of publishing sensations which is the modern book world. The book bloggers can do something as unique as the experience you had in that long ago dusty cornet of the school library – take you back to the word on the printed page and your own imagination.

Catheryn Kilgarriff

Further Reading

The blogs featured in this book include:

JUMPING ON THE BANDWAGON

Bookninja (www.bookninja.com)
Chasing Ray (www.chasingray.com)
Crockatt and Powell (www.crockattandpowell.blogspot.com)
Dovegreyreader (dovegreyreader.typepad.com)
Laila Lalami (www.lailalalami.com/blog)

ALTER EGOS OR INFLATED EGOS?

Ms Baroque (baroqueinhackney.blogspot.com)
Beatrice.com (www.beatrice.com)
Bibliophile Bullpen (bibliophilebullpen.blogspot.com)
Book/Daddy (www.artsjournal.com/bookdaddy)
Bookdwarf (www.bookdwarf.com)
Bookfox (www.bookfox.com)
Bookgasm (www.bookgasm.com)
Booksurfer (booksurfer.blogspot.com)
Buzzwords (www.3ammagazine.com/3am/buzzwords)
Confessions of an Idiosyncratic Mind (www.sarahweinman.com)
Cupcake (cupcakeseries.com)
Emerging Writers' Forum (www.breaktech.net/
emergingwritersforum/main.aspx
Galley Cat (mediabistro.com/galleycat)
Golden Rule Jones (www.goldenrulejones.com)
The Happy Booker (thehappybooker.blogs.com)
The Inner Minx (www.innerminx.blogspot.com)
Laurable (www.laurable.com)
The Literary Saloon (www.complete-review.com/saloon)
LitKicks (www.litkicks.com)
Mad Ink Beard (www.madinkbeard.com)
Mumpsimus (mumpsimus.blogspot.com)

Rakes Progress (rakesprogress.typepad.com)
ReadySteadyBook (www.readysteadybook.com)
Miss Snark (misssnark.blogspot.com)
Zyzzyva (www.zyzzyva.org)

BOOKSHOP AND BOOKSELLERS' BLOG

Mr B's Emporium of Reading Delights (mrbsemporium.com)
The Bookseller Crow on the Hill (www.booksellercrow.co.uk)
The Bookseller to the Stars (www.markfarley.blogspot.com)
Struggling Author (strugglingauthor.blogspot.com)

PUBLISHERS' BLOGS

Snowblog (www.snowbooks.com/weblog)
Me and My Big Mouth (meandmybigmouth.typepad.com/scottpack or see www.thefridayproject.co.uk)

FAN BLOGS, OBSESSIVES AND THE EXTREME

The Alienonline (www.thealienonline.net)
All About Romance (www.likesbooks.com)
The Baker Street Blog (www.bakerstreetblog.com)
Belle de Jour (belledejour-uk.blogspot.com)
Bookgasm (www.bookgasm.com)
Booksnbytes (www.booksnbytes.com)
Brontë Blog (bronteblog.blogspot.com)
CommanderBond.net (commanderbond.net)
Confessions of an Idiosyncratic Mind (www.sarahweinman.com)
Creatures of the Writes (www.creaturesofthewrite.com)
Crime Fiction Dossier (www.crimefictionblog.com)
Crime Spot (www.crimespot.net)
Crime Time (www.crimetime.co.uk)
Eurocrime (www.eurocrime.co.uk)
Gabrielle Faust (www.gabriellefaust.com)
Girl Detective (www.girl-detective.net)
The Good Girls Kill For Money Club (www.good-girls-kill.com)

The Groovy Age of Horror (groovyageofhorror.blogspot.com)
The Horror Blog (www.thehorrorblog.com)
I Heart Harlequin (www.iheartharlequinpresents.com)
The Internet Review of Science Fiction (www.irosf.com)
JK Rowling Official Website (www.jkrowling.com)
The James Bond 007 Blog (www.jamesbond007blog.com)
LA Noir (la-noir.blogspot.com)
The Leaky Cauldron (www.the-leaky-cauldron.org)
The Little Blog of Murder (www.thelittleblogofmurder.com)
Murderati (www.murderati.typepad.com)
The Mystery Chicks (themysterychicks.com)
Mystery File Blog (www.mysteryfile.com)
The Mystery Reader (www.themysteryreader.com)
Pulpetti (pulpetti.blogspot.com)
The Reader (thereaderonline.co.uk)
Romance: By The Blog (www.romancebytheblog.blogspot.com)
Romancing the Blog (www.romancingtheblog.com)
Romance Junkies (www.romancejunkies.com)
Shadowdark (www.shadowdark.com)
A Study in Sherlock (www.astudyinsherlock.net)
The Thrilling Detective Blog (www.thethrillingdetective.com)

THE LITERARY ESTABLISHMENT AND ITS BLOGS

Richard Charkin (charkinblog.macmillan.com)
Peter Stothard (timescolumns.typepad.com/stothard)

THE INTERNET AND ITS USES

Blog Everywhere (www.blogeverywhere.com)
Chad Post (www.rochester.edu/threepercent)
Riverbend (riverbendblog.blogspot.com)

DISSIDENTS AND REBELS

3:AM Magazine/Buzzwords (www.3ammagazine.com/3am/buzzwords)

Richard Hell (www.richardhell.com)
The Scarecrow (hodmandod.blogspot.com)
Social Disease (www.socialdisease.co.uk)

RIOT LIT AND THE LITERARY GROUPS WHO BLOG

The Believer (www.believermag.com)
Bookslut (www.bookslut.com)
The Brutalists (www.myspace.com/brutalists.com)
Girl on Demand (www.girlondemand.blogspot.com)
Grumpy Old Bookman (grumpyoldbookmanblogspot.com)
Litblog Co-op (lbc.typepad.com)
Maud Newton (www.maudnewton.com)
McSweeneys (store.mcsweeneys.net)
N+1 magazine (www.nplusonemag.com)
The OffBeat Generation (www.myspace.com/offbeatgeneration)
Outyourbackdoor (www.outyourbackdoor.com)
Pinky's Paperhouse (www.pinkyspaperhouse.com)
Return of the Reluctant (www.edrants.com)
Riot Lit Collective (riotlit.blogspot.com)
Slush Pile (www.slushpile.net)
Straight From the Fridge (www.upbondageupyours.blogspot.com)
Underground Literary Alliance (www.literaryrevolution.com)

BLOGGERS vs REVIEWS PAGES

Bookblog (bookblog.net)
The Complete Review (www.complete-review.com)
Counterbalance (counterbalance.typepad.com)
Critical Mass (www.criticalmass.com)
The Elegant Variation (marksarvas.blogs.com/elegvar)
Salon.com (www.salon.com)

BOOK BLOGS AND WRITERS

The Book Bar (visit.thebookbar.com)
Book Slam (www.bookslam.com)

Francesca Beard (www.francescabeard.com)
Toby Litt (www.tobylitt.com)
Jeff Vandemeer (vanderworld.blogspot.com)
Jeannette Winterson (www.jeanettewinterson.com)
Me and My Big Mouth/Scott Pack (meandmybigmouth.typepad.com/scottpack or see www.thefridayproject.co.uk)
Neil Gaiman (www.neilgaiman.com)
Noam Chomsky (www.noamchomsky.info)
Random Jottings of a Book Lover (randomjottings.typepad.com)
Snowbooks (www.snowbooks.com/weblog)
Susan Hill (www.susan-hill.com)
Toby Litt (www.tobylitt.com)

BOOKSELLING AND THE NET REVOLUTION

Audio Books Corner (www.audiobookscorner.com)
Audio Books Online (www.audiobooksonline.com)
Barnes & Noble (www.barnesandnoble.com)
Black Butterfly Review (www.blackbutterflyreview.com)
BlackRefer.com (www.blackrefer.com)
Blogger.com (www.blogger.com)
Book Brain (www.bookbrain.co.uk)
Books.co.uk (www.books.co.uk)
Frontlist Books (www.frontlist.com)
icue (i-cue.co.uk)
Kelkoo (www.kelkoo.com)
The Kids Window (www.thekidswindow.com)
Laila Lalami (www.lailalalami.com)
Listen2online (www.listen2online.co.uk)
Live Journal (www.livejournal.com)
The Millions Blog (www.themillionsblog.com)
Novel Arts (www.novelarts.com)
Romance Design Community (www.romancedesigns.com)
Romance at Heart magazine (www.romanceatheart.com)

Salon.com (www.salon.com)
Spike Magazine (www.spikemagazine.com)